Bruton
in Selwood

Bruton
in Selwood
A HISTORY

Andrew Pickering

To Rory, Louie, Eleanor and Lyndon
There and back again

First published in the United Kingdom in 2022
by The Hobnob Press,
8 Lock Warehouse, Severn Road, Gloucester GL1 2GA
www.hobnobpress.co.uk

© Andrew Pickering, text and images, 2021, 2022

The Author hereby asserts his moral rights to be identified as the Author of the Work.

All rights reserved. No part of this publication may be reproduced, stored in a retrieval system, or transmitted in any form or by any means, electronic, mechanical, photocopying, recording or otherwise, without the prior permission of the publisher and copyright holder.

British Library Cataloguing in Publication Data
A catalogue record for this book is available from the British Library

ISBN 978-1-914407-09-3

Typeset in Chaparral Pro, 11/14 pt
Typesetting and origination by John Chandler

CONTENTS

INTRODUCTION vii
ACKNOWLEDGEMENTS xii

1 BEFORE BRUTON 1
   Of Stone, Bronze and Iron 1
   Romano-Bruton 3
   The Frontier Era, AD 410–658 6

2 MEDIEVAL BRUTON 10
   Bruton Begins 10
   Alfred's Tower 12
   Bruton Manor 14
   Bruton Abbey 15
   Bruton Town 17
   The Church of St Mary the Virgin 19
   Agriculture, Trade and Industry 22
   National Affairs 24

3 REFORMATIONS AND REBELLIONS: BRUTON IN THE SIXTEENTH AND SEVENTEENTH CENTURIES 25
   Population and Public Health 25
   The Reformation 27
   Stephan Batman 28
   The Berkeley Family 30
   Bruton's Civil War 35
   Bruton and the Monmouth Rebellion 37
   Town Life 38
   The Poor 39
   Hugh Sexey 41
   The Witches of Brewham 45
   Bruton's Seventeenth-Century Witchcraft Trial 48
   Bruton's Early Quaker Community 51

4 POVERTY AND PLENTY: BRUTON IN THE EIGHTEENTH AND NINETEENTH CENTURIES — 53

- Population and Public Health — 53
- Hard Times — 56
- Work — 59
- Communications — 64
- Some Literary Connections — 69
- The Hobhouse Family — 71
- Schools — 72
- Church and Chapel — 76
- Self-help and Philanthropy — 77
- Pubs and Public Amenities — 79
- Entertainment — 81
- Law and Order — 83

5 BRUTON IN MODERN TIMES — 85

- Around and About — 85
- Redlynch House — 86
- Floods — 88
- Bruton at War — 89
- Artist in Residence: Ernst Müller-Blensdorf — 92
- Writer in Residence: John Steinbeck — 96
- Modern Times: Change and Continuity — 99

BIBLIOGRAPHY — 106
INDEX — 111

INTRODUCTION

The town of Briweton to the marquet crosse standith yn Selwod. And so doth the abbay on the other ripe of the ryver. The ryver of Briwe risith in Selwod at a place caullid Briweham 3 miles from Brutun.

(John Leland, 1542)

THE HISTORY OF Bruton is commemorated in the fascinating collection of objects housed in the town's museum on the High Street at the heart of the medieval market-town. It is further encapsulated in the architecture and fabric of the old buildings that surround it, the unique history of each reflecting much of what defines that of the town at large. Let us consider just one of these by way of an introduction.

Next door to the museum is the popular restaurant and bakery 'At the Chapel'. The building seems to have been constructed in the 1750s by Sir Charles Berkeley of the eminent family that had dominated its civic affairs ever since it acquired Bruton Abbey and its estate following its dissolution in 1539. It occupied the site of one of the town's many inns, the Swan, which had been established at least as early as 1669 and which was up for let in 1746, advertised as having stables, a brewhouse, a malthouse and 'everything convenient for a House of entertainment'. By 1750 the town's main business was the production of cloth, traditionally woollens and later silk, and Berkeley's building was a factory fulfilling one or more stages of the complex process of production. By the end of the eighteenth century the great age of woollen cloth production in the town had passed and in around 1803 it was converted into a Congregationalist chapel, known as the Union Chapel. As such it played a part in the rich history of post-Reformation non-conformism and evangelism in the town, which includes the persecution of seventeenth-century Quakers, visits by eminent preachers, including John Wesley, and the arrival, in 1848, of the West End Methodist Chapel. In turn the Chapel's schoolrooms contributed their part to another central plank in Bruton's history: the provision of education in multiple schools across the course of more than half a millennium. After its closure in 1969 the Chapel developed in line with the flourishing of the arts in and around the

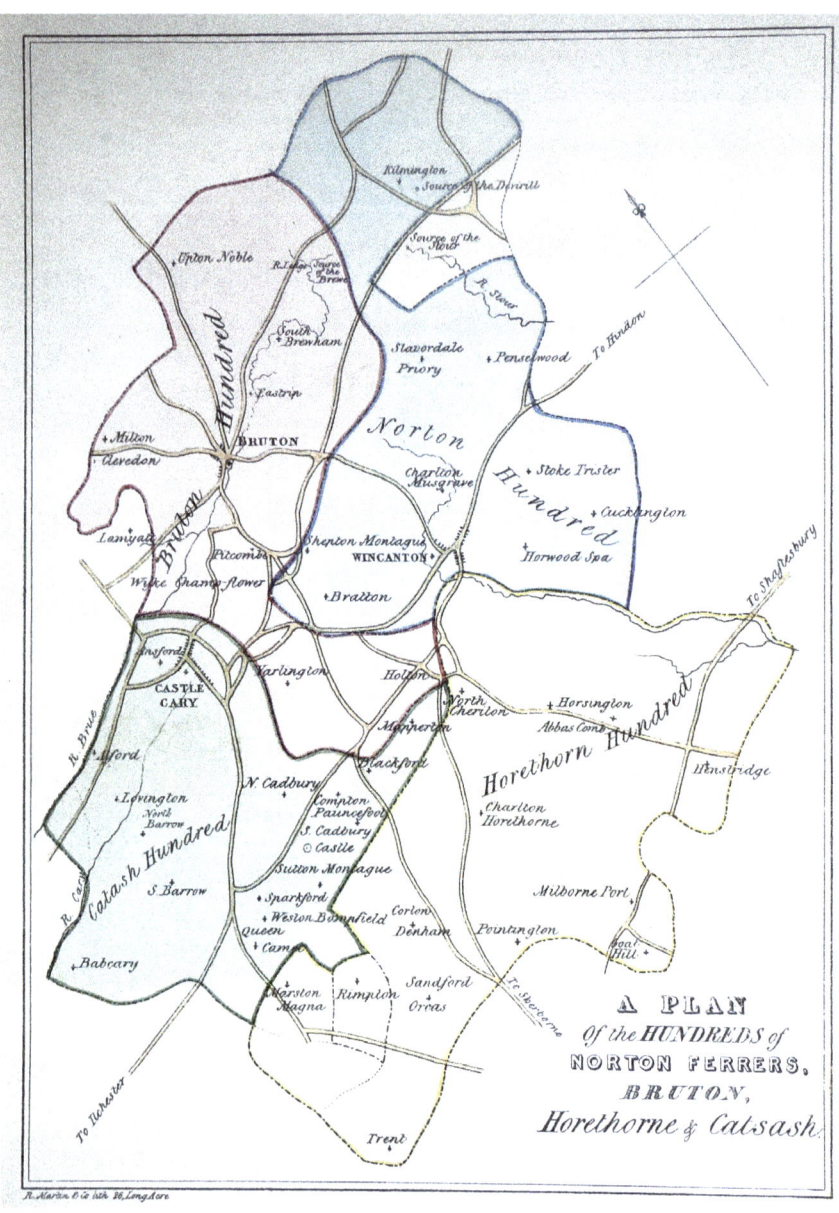

A plan of the hundreds of Norton Ferris, Bruton, Horethorne and Catsash, 1832. (Lithograph by R. Martin and Co.)

town since the mid-twentieth century. The premises, known for a time as 'Atlantis', housed a sculptor's workshop and a professional recording studio

INTRODUCTION

before being converted by the present owners back into a contemporary 'house of entertainment', and a very successful one at that, which both reflects and has greatly contributed to Bruton's present reputation as a cultural hub and provider of high-end hospitality.

In compiling this history of Bruton and the surrounding parishes that formed the historic Bruton Hundred, everything published so far that has had much to say about the area has been considered. The single most valuable archaeological resource is Somerset's Historic Environment Record. For analyses of early medieval texts and other evidence in the era in which both Somerset and Bruton were born, the work of Michael Costen has proved most useful. The starting place for the medieval history of the town – of the buildings and institutions and the people who lived, worshipped and worked therein – is 'The Bruton Hundred' entry in John Collinson's *The History and Antiquities of the County of Somerset* (1791). This also provides a glimpse of life in the town in Georgian times. Peter Randell's extensive investigations among the parish registers, and judicial and institutional records, have enriched this book with details of the social history of the town from the early modern period to the present day. His *Life and Times of Hugh Sexey* and two volumes on over 500 years of education in the town are the definitive texts on these subjects. For the history of more recent times, the recollections of residents during the Second World War,

Bruton High Street, c.1905; Bruton Museum is located in the arched building on the right.

Early map of Bruton (pre-1848).

gathered together on behalf of the Royal British Legion in 2005, have been plundered for information and anecdotes. The original *Dictionary of National Biography* and its modern counterpart, the *Oxford Dictionary of National Biography*, have been invaluable in telling the stories of eminent individuals associated with Bruton. For those not profiled in the ODNB the team at Bruton Museum over the past couple of decades has raised awareness of the silversmith Gabriel Felling, the greatly underrated sculptor Ernst Blensdorf, and the surprising history of Bruton's intimate relationship with the great American novelist John Steinbeck.

INTRODUCTION

The first detailed history of the town, long out of print, was Phyllis Couzens' *Bruton in Selwood*, published in 1968. This inspirational work was the first to consider Bruton in its wider Selwood context and it is with affection and gratitude that this history shares its title. Since then the town's story has been told in The *Victoria History of the County of Somerset*: Volume VII (1999), which remains the key text against which the veracity of all other accounts can and should be checked. The history of the church is covered in the scholarly *St Mary the Virgin, Bruton: A Brief History* by John Bishton. In the 1990s Colin Clarke, a long-serving curator of Bruton Museum, produced several interesting and copiously illustrated volumes on aspects of Bruton's history, including a transcription, with a useful commentary, of the diaries of Josiah Jackson of Durslade Farm, thus bringing to light an invaluable source for the social history of Bruton towards the end of Victoria's reign. Aspects of its late-twentieth-century history have been gleaned from a wide range of ephemera and conversations with people who have lived their lives in the town. Ken Dominey's memoir of growing up in Bruton has been particularly informative. The findings of staff and students of the Department of Architecture and Spatial Design at London Metropolitan University were published as a fascinating volume by Bruton Museum in 2009. For the convenience of future researchers, a full bibliography detailing these and other sources can be found at the end of this book.

Andrew Pickering
Chairman of the Committee,
Bruton Museum

Bruton Museum

ACKNOWLEDGEMENTS

THE AUTHOR is grateful to everyone who has permitted the use of their images for this publication. The older and unattributed images are, to the best of his knowledge, in the public domain and available for reproduction under the terms and conditions of Creative Commons licences. He is grateful also to curator, Jackie Brooks, and fellow committee members of Bruton Museum for their support in this project, in particular Elisabeth Balfour for her expert proofing of the text. John Chandler of Hobnob Press provided unstinting support in undertaking further checks, designing, typesetting and publishing this book. Grateful thanks are offered to those organisations and individuals whose support has helped the museum to remain viable in very challenging times; these include its members and anonymous sponsors, Bruton Town Council, South Somerset District Council, and South-West Heritage. He and the museum are especially grateful to good friends and benefactors at Hauser & Wirth for their generosity and enthusiasm for safe-guarding Bruton's precious heritage.

1
BEFORE BRUTON

Of Stone, Bronze and Iron

THE EARLIEST EVIDENCE of human activity in the vicinity of Bruton includes a scatter of prehistoric flint tools and evidence of flint-tool making, discovered at Holywater Copse opposite Godminster Farmhouse early in the twentieth century, and what might be the remains of a Bronze Age barrow on a hill south-east of Bruton at Redlynch between Dropping Lane Farm and Redlynch Farm. Potentially rather older is the intriguing impression of a possible Neolithic long barrow showing as a cropmark in an aerial photograph, recorded in 2010, a couple of miles to the north of the town, close to Higher Greenscombe Farm. Prehistoric finds in the area include a flat copper alloy axe-head, identifiable typologically as dating from the early Bronze Age; it was found to the south-east of Cook's Farm in Brewham. It was reported under the Portable Antiquities Scheme and a photographic record of the axe has been archived even though it and its owners are thought to have left the country. In the same parish an earlier, Neolithic, polished stone axe was found in the mid-twentieth century at Cards Farm. At Shave Farm, also in Brewham, a curious stone in a former orchard has been interpreted as a possible prehistoric standing stone – a very rare feature in the region.

Overlooking Bruton, to the north-east of the town, is the archaeologically rich landscape of Creech Hill. Here two assemblages of tools and flint cores, of supposed Neolithic or Bronze Age antiquity, were collected and presented to Taunton Museum (now The Museum of Somerset) between 1901 and 1909. At the west end of Creech Hill can be seen the remains of a small, univallate (i.e. single bank and ditch) 'hillfort' structure, probably dating from the early Iron Age or even the late Bronze Age. The term could be something of a misnomer for what might have served as a stock enclosure as opposed to being a place of settlement, refuge and defence. On the west side of the enclosure are the remains of another supposed late Neolithic or early Bronze Age barrow. To the north of Creech Hill is the much more impressive multivallated Small Down hillfort, which encloses a cemetery of at least eleven, possibly as many as fourteen, such barrows.

In 2016 evidence was found suggesting a late Iron Age or Romano-British settlement at Pitcombe. Elsewhere in the region, clusters of Iron Age pottery and associated features have been found at Castle Cary, and Penselwood is recognised through a range of finds as a place of relatively intensive activity in the Bronze and Iron Ages. Somewhere in the vicinity of Penselwood a middle Bronze Age rapier was discovered, now kept at the Blackmore Museum in Salisbury. An incomplete Bronze Age torc from Pen Pits was given to Taunton Museum in the middle of the nineteenth century. Richard Tabor, who has spent a lifetime researching and exploring the landscape around South Cadbury, identified some intriguing cropmarks at Shepton Montague; these include a ring ditch 20 metres in diameter and 'an almost cursus-like' linear feature.

With so little evidence of pre-Roman Conquest activity in the area it is difficult to identify exactly where the people who left these faint footprints behind actually lived. No doubt people lived at Smalldown at some point and it is reasonable to presume a farmstead or even more substantial settlement was established within or close to the enclosure on Creech Hill at Milton Clevedon. Nevertheless, the *manner* of their lives is understood, not least through the extraordinary archaeological record of the famous Iron Age lake villages close to Glastonbury and, even closer, the great developed hillfort of South Cadbury. They lived in roundhouses of various designs – the remains of some of which have survived in the anaerobic environment of the Somerset Levels. At South Cadbury, where the timbers have long since rotted, they leave their mark as so many post-holes, gullies, and hearths. Other structures of four or six posts are found here too – small rectilinear features that have been interpreted as raised granaries or stores for other resources. Although they have not yet been found, it is reasonable to suppose such structures once stood in the upper reaches of the Brue valley and on the hills above it.

In the second century AD the Greek commentator Ptolemy listed the 'tribes' that occupied Britain at the time of the Roman Conquest. For the Durotriges – the people of what would become Dorset and south-east

The River Brue, c.1924.

Somerset – the Selwood ridge was an obvious northern border and the River Brue that flows beneath it created another natural border in the flooded moorland on the northern side of the Polden Hills. The distribution of 'Durotrigan' style pottery and, especially, coinage (first appearing in the first century AD), has helped archaeologists construct their hypothetical maps of the tribal territory, locating Bruton on this northern boundary. For many years this has been construed as a firmly united polity focused upon the region's great hillforts such as South Cadbury and Ham Hill, and dominated by the incumbents of the greatest of them all – Maiden Castle on the edge of Dorchester. Its ascendancy up to the time of Caesar's invasions in 55 and 54 BC was in part due to its presumed domination of continental trade via Hengistbury Head (Christchurch) and Poole Harbour. More recently Martin Papworth has suggested this could have been no more than a fragile economic and military alliance.

Romano-Bruton

WHILE HE WAS staying in Bruton in 1959 the famous American novelist John Steinbeck was fascinated by the work presently being undertaken nearby by King's School boys and a local archaeologist: the excavation of Creech Hill. He told his editor, 'Every Wednesday afternoon they excavate on Creech Hill about five miles from here – real knowledgeable boys 15 to 17. They invited me for next Wednesday and I wouldn't miss it.' A few days later he wrote of visiting the hill where the boys were working 'under the direction of good people from the British Museum'. He spoke of a Neolithic fort overlaid by an Iron Age fort 'and on top of all a Roman temple'.

The site he described is also known as Fox Covert, the univallate enclosure mentioned above. In 1956 a short report written by Sheila Watts was published in *Proceedings of the University of Bristol Speleological Society* which declares it was 'found' in 1955. Even more exciting was the recent discovery of 'a Roman building, perhaps a temple' found close by on Lamyatt Beacon on the south-west spur of Creech Hill.

This important site was partially excavated between 1955 and 1960 by Crystal Bennett, an archaeologist who lived in Bruton. Here Bennett and her team of boys from King's School found pottery, hundreds of third- and fourth-century coins, a small rock-cut chamber, a great quantity of oyster shells, two skeletons and several bronze figurines including two depicting Mercury, and others Minerva, Mars, Hercules and a priest. The unwelcome activities of treasure-hunters (locals speak of finds in private hands in Bruton and elsewhere today) prompted Roger Leech to complete the excavation of the site in 1973.

The Lamyatt Temple Mercury figurine photographed soon after its discovery; replicas of this and several more figures from the temple are on display in Bruton Museum. (Photo: O. Fein)

Steinbeck engaged in his own minor excavations around the cottage he was renting on the south side of Bruton at Discove, exploring the remains of the five demolished cottages that once stood beside his own. Finding rubble that included some thin red bricks that he thought might be Roman, he concluded that Discove was a Roman religious centre, 'possibly dedicated to Dis Pater and perhaps built on an older ring'. His ideas were not as far-fetched as they might seem. According to Collinson, a Roman tessellated pavement was found there in 1711 at an unrecorded site, and, nearby, 'in Lord Fitzharding's grounds near the town of Brewton', some time before 1714, a mid-second-century AD Roman 'pig' of Mendip lead turned up in the parish. Its inscription read, 'IMP DVOR AVG ANTONINI ET VERI ARMENIACORUM', which has been translated as 'property of the two August Emperors Antoninus and Verus, conquerors of Armenia [i.e. Brittany]'. Bennett identified what she considered to be a stretch of Roman road close to Godminster Wood between the town and Discove, and a Roman hoard of twenty-one coins was discovered at Godminster Farm and acquired by Taunton Museum in the late 1950s.

In 1836 William Phelps recorded the then recent discovery in 1834 of stone roofing tiles and Roman coins at nearby Bratton Seymour. These were probably fragments of the Roman villa site that would be identified on the Hobhouse family estate, in a field known as Blacklands, close to Discove. Following the chance discovery of a mosaic floor in 1966, it too was excavated by Bennett in 1968, just a few years after Steinbeck met her on Creech Hill. Ceramic evidence from the site indicates an initial

Engraving showing St. Mary's and Bruton from the south; the distinctive point of Lamyatt Beacon, site of a Roman temple, is in the background.

mid-third-century AD construction with later developments including a late-fourth-century cobbled floor. A second mosaic was discovered which is centred upon the head and shoulders image of an individual that might be a portrait of the goddess Diana. The high status of the site is further amplified by what is interpreted as a probable hypocaust heating system.

Another possible villa site, a couple of miles downstream from Bruton, has been identified on the south side of East Hill in the parish of Ditcheat. It first appeared in the archaeological record in 1985 as 'a series of strange parallel compartments' captured in aerial photographs. A more certain villa site is one close to the Brook Inn in the heart of the village of Ditcheat. Of Romano-Britons in the centre of Bruton, however, there is no clear archaeological indication. Considerable quantities of densely packed, deeply buried oyster shells, a feature of the Lamyatt temple site, have been found in town-centre gardens and it is highly probable future excavations will reveal artefacts dating to the Roman era. In 2005 a stretch of what has been interpreted as a Roman road or late Iron Age trackway was discovered at Grove Farm in Pitcombe. Geophysics and a test-pit excavation have revealed another at Yarlington.

The Frontier Era, AD 410–658

Between the latter part of the fourth century AD and the end of the first quarter of the fifth, in the words of the historian Robin Fleming, 'Britain not only fell out of the empire but lost everything that made it Roman'. The history of the immediate aftermath of the severing of links with Rome is shrouded in the mystery of, effectively, a non-literate age and told through the oblique lens of later commentators, notably Gildas who probably composed *De excidio et conquestu Britanniae* ('On the ruin and conquest of Britain') at the start of the sixth century, and the Anglo-Saxon monk Bede, whose HISTORIA ECCLESIASTICA GENTIS ANGLORUM ('Ecclesiastical History of the English People'), drawing heavily on Gildas, was completed in 731. In this historically 'dark age' the evidence of archaeology remains of paramount importance.

A literal reading of the early sources indicates an imploding Britain as petty rulers fought among themselves to hold their own in the face of anarchy. Towns decayed and villas were abandoned; production of pottery and metal goods ceased. Their problems were exacerbated by a terrible plague, perhaps as severe as the Black Death, which swept through the whole Roman world in around 443. In the middle of that century, one tyrannical and mighty lord, Vortigern, so the story goes, invited Germanic mercenaries into his realm. Led by two brothers, Hengist and Horsa, they soon rebelled against their paymaster and the Anglo-Saxon conquest of Britain was begun. Having subjugated the south-east the Saxons headed west.

While this is not the place to engage in the debate regarding invasion and migration hypotheses, nor the controversy surrounding numbers of migrants and the scale of displacement of resident Britons, there is good reason to suppose that the ridge of Selwood and its great forest then known as the *Coit Mawr* – the landscape on the northern and eastern sides of Bruton – represented an important frontier which, for a time, held strong against hostile incomers.

It is through its close proximity to the great hillfort at South Cadbury, just beyond the parish of Yarlington at the southern tip of the Bruton Hundred and visible from the higher ground at various points in the town, that Bruton most obviously falls into the orbit of King Arthur, the legendary victor in the battle of Mount Badon fought against the Saxons in about AD 500. The earliest surviving text linking Cadbury Castle to what was probably already a long-established tradition that this was Arthur's headquarters dates from the 1530s, when John Leland, 'sub-librarian' in one of Henry VIII's royal libraries, visited East Somerset. In his *Itinerary* (1542) he recorded his arrival at Bruton Abbey after a perusal of the religious houses of Wells and Glastonbury. On his way from Bruton to the abbey at Sherborne he took a detour to explore South Cadbury, presumably because of its Arthurian associations, something that would have been of particular interest to his royal master who claimed a Welsh/British ancestry that included the legendary king. Of the hillfort's substantial ditches, earthen ramparts and rubble walls, he wrote, 'The only information local people can offer is that they have heard that Arthur frequently came to Camelot.'

The excavations of South Cadbury hillfort, directed by Leslie Alcock in the late 1960s, revealed that it had been reoccupied and massively refortified in the 'Arthurian' fifth and sixth centuries AD. Whoever controlled the hill at this time was clearly a person of considerable local importance and power – a warlord, chieftain or king perhaps. Its high status in the period is further confirmed by the archaeologists' discoveries of exotic eastern Mediterranean 'Tintagel ware' pottery sherds at the site, imported via the riverine trade centred upon nearby Ilchester. It commanded a powerful position close to the Fosse Way and on the south side of what was probably an important trackway from west to east on the line of the modern A303. Cadbury provided an ideal base for the mustering of British warriors to counter the advances of the Saxon invaders attempting to cross the Selwood ridge. Hindsight makes a clash of British and Anglo-Saxon arms in the immediate vicinity of Bruton, nestled as it is beneath the ridge, sandwiched between it and Cadbury Castle, seem inevitable.

Archaeological evidence does not seem to contradict the implication of historical sources that after Badon the Anglo-Saxon advance westwards ceased for, according to Gildas, at least several decades. Michael Costen has postulated that so long as those in the emerging kingdom of Wessex on the eastern (Wiltshire) side of the Selwood ridge remained relatively under-organised those on the western (Bruton) side were secure in the shadow of South Cadbury until, in the seventh century, 'the rise of an Anglo-Saxon polity based upon predatory warfare and led by warrior princes and their land-hungry kinsmen sealed the fate of this post-Roman society'.

In 658, according to the *Anglo-Saxon Chronicle* (or, at least, a modern translation thereof),

> Cenwalh [king of Wessex] fought at Penselwood with the Welsh [i.e. British], and they put them to flight to the Parret. This battle was fought three years after he had come from East Anglia [...]

The place name in the original in fact is '*peonnum*' but almost certainly should be regarded as Penselwood, just four miles to the east of Bruton, where the ancient borders of Wiltshire, Dorset and Somerset, in Selwood, meet. By now it would appear, according to the archaeological record, Cadbury Castle had been abandoned and this point of entry no longer enjoyed the protection of its garrison. The way was open for Saxon adventurers to advance on the main prize – Ilchester. Unfortunately, the historicity of the battle has not yet been, and probably never will be, proved but there is some support for an incursion by Saxon warriors in the form of nine roughly contemporary burials at Queen Camel, halfway between South Cadbury and Ilchester, one of which included a Germanic-style sword. Of course, the exact site of the supposed battle is unknown, but it can be presumed it was fought on, or very close to, the supposed ancient highway that preceded the A303. This event of 658 – Bruton's local battle – is of great significance in the county's history in marking the first decisive blow in the Saxon conquest of what would subsequently be called Somerset. To paraphrase Costen, the frontier era was over and Somerset was well on its way to emerging in a recognisable form.

2
MEDIEVAL BRUTON

Bruton Begins

BRUTON IS A town of Saxon origin, established around the site of the present church of St Mary the Virgin on the southern bank of the Brue. If there was a significant community in the vicinity already, Michael Costen has suggested that another great estate, in addition to that of South Cadbury, could have been centred upon Lamyatt, the hilltop location of the old Roman temple. Following the decline of Cadbury, might men have been assembled here to ride out against the Saxon invaders and fight at Penselwood? Even though the archaeological record for the period is slight it is probable there was already some kind of pre-Saxon settlement in the Brue valley below. Costen has remarked on the growing body of evidence supporting the notion that *wic* place-names, as in Bruton's adjacent Wyke Champflower, denote Romano-British farmsteads and hamlets.

An early reference to a church at Bruton appears in William of Malmesbury's twelfth-century hagiography of St Aldhelm (d. 709/710), the first bishop of Sherborne, the abbot of Malmesbury, and one of the greatest churchmen of his age, who, allegedly, had it built at the start of the eighth century and dedicated it to St Peter. The name 'Godminster' implies there was some kind of religious centre on the southern side

Anglo-Saxon sword (replica) in Bruton Museum. (Photo: Jackie Brooks)

St Mary's and the Abbey Playing Fields in 2021, site of the medieval abbey and supposed location of the original Saxon settlement. (Photo: Author)

of Bruton. This might have been the site of St Peter's Church and its proximity to a place known as 'Holy Well' might indicate an association with an even earlier, perhaps pre-Christian, ritual site. A second church in Bruton, dedicated to the Virgin Mary, was said to have a marble altar brought from Rome by Aldhelm which he gave to Ine, King of Wessex from 688 to 726. Various chapels were built in the vicinity of St Mary's in the following centuries. It has been proposed that the site of the original settlement at Bruton was on the south side of the river, centred on the church. Until a contemporary cemetery site is found it will be impossible to say who lived there, whether they were local Britons or Saxon incomers. And even if burial evidence does come to light the evidence is likely to prove inconclusive.

In March 1984 a Saxon-era sword, probably of ninth-century antiquity, was discovered in the east of the parish at Sheephouse Farm in Cogley Wood during the excavations for the dam that was to be constructed there by Wessex Water. It is now kept at the Museum of

Somerset but a reconstruction of the original, made in 1986, can be seen in Bruton Museum. It is classified as a 'type L' sword, of which fifteen have been found in Britain. Although more have been found in Norway, many, if not all, of these are thought to have been of British origin. Thus it can be presumed to be an 'English' sword and quite possibly one intended for the defence of Wessex in the era of the attempts by Danish Vikings to conquer the kingdom during the reign of Alfred the Great (871–899).

Alfred's Tower

High on the ridge at this southern end of Selwood Forest, in the parish of South Brewham, Alfred's Tower, also known as Stourton Tower, marks the supposed site of King Alfred's meeting at Easter 878 (or 879 according to some versions of the *Anglo-Saxon Chronicle*) with the men of Somerset, Wiltshire and Hampshire at a local landmark known as Egbert's Stone. Together they went on to fight and defeat a Viking army led by the Dane Guthrum at Ethandune (subsequently known as Edington), and thus saved Alfred's kingdom of Wessex. The men of Dorset, who did not meet their king at Egbert's Stone, were entrusted, it can be supposed, with the task of defending the kingdom from a seaborne Viking assault in the south.

Since Christmas 877, when the Vikings invaded from the north and he was forced to flee from his winter abode at Chippenham, Alfred had been hiding out in the heart of the Somerset marshes at Athelney. From here his men harried the Danes in their camp, which was probably situated on the Polden ridge overlooking Athelney in the southern moors. This was just a few hours' march to his rendezvous in Selwood Forest, where the borders of the western shires of his kingdom met at Egbert's Stone. The location of this landmark is uncertain, but one strong contender is a remote standing stone in the parish of Penselwood. The site of the battle of Ethandune is also unproven; traditional histories, which erroneously maintain that the Vikings subsequently retreated to Chippenham, place it at Edington near Westbury in Wiltshire, but others envisage Alfred returning to the Somerset Levels to take on the Vikings at another village called Edington – this one in the Polden Hills. A Somerset location would certainly make good sense, since the Vikings were undoubtedly in the vicinity of Athelney in the weeks leading up to the Easter of 878, and the

Alfred's Tower. (Lithograph, c. 1875)

treaty directly after the battle was sealed by ceremonies at Aller, very close to Athelney, and at Wedmore, directly to the north of the Polden Hills.

Constructed on Kingsettle Hill in the eighteenth century, the tower is in the parish of Brewham on the south-eastern edge of the Bruton Hundred. It was commissioned as both a memorial and a spectacular viewing platform by the banker Henry Hoare II, of nearby Stourhead House, and, from 1776, the owner of Bruton manor. Designed by Henry Flitcroft and finished in 1772, it is triangular in shape and made of over a million bricks with stone dressings; it rises to a height of about 49 metres (160 feet). 205 steps provide access to its embattled parapet overlooking three counties: Somerset, Wiltshire and Dorset. Close by, the source of the Brue, which runs westward through Brewham and on to Bruton, is identified by the remains of a monument constructed in 1847.

A ten-foot-tall statue of Alfred is embedded above the gothic-arched entrance of the south-eastern face of the tower. Directly below the statue is a decayed hyperbolic inscription commemorating the king in the heroic guise in which he was perceived by Georgian patriots celebrating their proud Anglo-Saxon Germanic past and present:

> ALFRED THE GREAT
> AD 879 on this Summit
> Erected his Standard
> Against Danish Invaders
> To him We owe The Origin of Juries
> The Establishment of a Militia
> The Creation of a Naval Force
> ALFRED The Light of a Benighted Age
> Was a Philosopher and a Christian
> The Father of his People
> The Founder of the English
> MONARCHY and LIBERTY

Bruton Manor

BRUTON HAD A mint at different times in the tenth and eleventh centuries. In 1066 four estates formed the parish, of which that held by King Edward was much the largest. It seems to have been dispersed by

Henry I, in the first part of the twelfth century, to William de Mohun, the Earl of Somerset from 1141, who already had the estate of Brewham and is supposed, by Couzens, to have lived at Colinshayes where the borders of the two estates met. The Luttrell family later acquired it as the nominal lords and patrons of the priory.

The population of the estate of Bruton at the time of the Domesday Book was around 250–300. Presumably regarded as Crown property at the time of William the Conqueror, it had been passed on to the Tancarville family by 1133. This estate, changing and expanding through the Middle Ages, was transferred to the canons of Bruton's new priory in the mid-twelfth century. They held it until 1539 when it reverted to the Crown.

The manor of Milton Clevedon was held by the Lovell family from the time of the reign of Henry II. Though ancient it was not listed in the Domesday Book and can thus be presumed to be a settlement of Norman origin. North Court, the manor house for North Brewham, once stood on the site of Batt's Farm.

Bruton Abbey

Both of Bruton's Saxon churches were still standing in the twelfth century. One, it was believed, served a pre-Conquest religious community established by Algar, the earl of Cornwall, although there is

Bruton Abbey Wall, c. 1965; the wall might be of fifteenth-century origin and features blocked quatrefoil panels and carriage arch, window, and doorway.

Left: Doulting stone head in Bruton Museum – probably a relic of the medieval church or priory. (Photo: Author)
Right: Architectural fragments and other material excavated in the Rectory garden in 2018. (Photo: Author)

no mention of a monastic community in Bruton's Domesday Book entry. Other places of worship included, in the twelfth century, a chapel dedicated to St George somewhere in Patwell Street. This was let for secular purposes by 1550 and had been converted into three tenements by 1699.

The subsequent Augustinian abbey, established in 1511, was formerly a priory 'of black canons, on the ruin of a more ancient religious house for Benedictine monks', according to Collinson, founded in 1142 by de Mohun's son, also named William, the Earl of Somerset. Tenth- or eleventh-century pottery has been found in excavations at the site of the subsequent abbey. In the reign of Henry VIII, William Gilbert, prior and, subsequently, abbot of Bruton, greatly improved the abbey and the king granted it the right to hold two annual fairs. All that remains of it, and the magnificent mansion into which it evolved under the ownership of the Berkeley family, is a massive buttressed wall enclosing the park in which their home was built. Although trees were planted in the deer park, ponds were dug, and lawns and walks were laid out in the 1760s, the Abbey/mansion buildings became a quarry after the childless last Baron Berkeley died in 1773. The property was purchased in 1776 by Henry Hoare, who had made his fortune in banking. Sir Richard Hoare of Stourhead had no need for a further mansion and it was dismantled and sold as building stone. Little remained by 1789. Consequently many houses and other

MEDIEVAL BRUTON

structures in the town centre contain elements of medieval carved stone. Between 1822 and 1823 Abbey Stables, the buildings against the precinct wall, were replaced by Sir Richard Colt Hoare with a home for the minister of St Mary's Church, the 'perpetual curate' as then titled, a position often held by the headmaster of King's School.

Tradition has it that Bruton's best-known landmark, the Dovecote, was built to serve the canons of the abbey, although the 200 nesting boxes on its inside appear to be a later addition. An alternative explanation is that it was built as a prospect tower in the seventeenth century by the Berkeleys. On its eastern side a low linear mound identifies the remains of a medieval man-made rabbit warren, known as a pillow mound, which can certainly be presumed to have helped fill the abbey's larders as well as providing fur for garments. The remains of what are usually presumed to be the Abbot's flight of three fishponds, unless they are marl pits, can be seen close by.

The Dovecote. (Photo: Author)

Bruton Town

THE MEDIEVAL SETTLEMENT, seemingly planned, was centred upon the market-place and buildings ran along the east end of the High Street, down Patwell Street towards the church, along Quaperlake Street, almost as far as what is now Uphills, and halfway up Coombe Street. Outlying buildings included a number of structures at West End. Nearby the earlier east wing of Priory House is an intriguing late medieval jettied

Priory House.

building which may have served as a guest-house and/or the court-house for Bruton Priory. It is decorated with clues denoting its fifteenth-century builder. These include the letters 'I H' for Iohn (John) Henton, and 'P B' for Prior of Bruton. His name is also identifiable in the images of a hen and a 'tun' – the common term for a barrel in former times. Dendrochronology has produced mid-fifteenth-century dates for the felling of timbers used in the building of numbers 16–18 and 20 High Street, matched in period by the style of their timber construction. A building in Amors Barton has been dated to the early fifteenth century.

Prior Henton's motif on the wall of Priory House. (Photo: Author)

An attractive single-arch bridge over the river, dating back to the fifteenth century, provides a pedestrian crossing a short distance to the west of Church Bridge. Bow Bridge is now better known locally as the Packhorse Bridge, which is a generic term for ancient narrow bridges with low parapets that date back to times when bulky goods were carried in panniers on the back of a horse. It is sometimes assumed that this bridge was built specifically to provide access to the town centre for the canons of Bruton Priory.

Bow Bridge, also known as the Packhorse Bridge, looking east towards Church Bridge. The Crown Inn, visible here at the north end of Church Bridge, has long-since been demolished.

THE CHURCH OF ST MARY THE VIRGIN

AS WELL AS a deeply satisfying architecture on the outside, St Mary's contains many features of note on the inside, including an excellent carved roof and striking stained-glass windows. It is unusual in having two towers – the smaller of the two is thought to date from the mid-fourteenth century; the tower at the western end was almost certainly completed in the mid-fifteenth. Whatever stood there before seems to have been entirely swept away in its great Perpendicular rebuild. Surprisingly perhaps, such extravagant ecclesiastical rebuilding was not at all unusual in the era of the Wars of the Roses. Bruton was unscathed by these wars; the closest involvement perhaps being when a part of Henry VI's wife Margaret of Anjou's army came this way, seeking to divert the army of her Yorkist enemy, Edward IV, before her final defeat at Tewkesbury in 1471.

Above: The remarkable eighteenth-century reredos in the chancel of St Mary's. (Photo: Author)
Left: A thirteenth-century chest of uncertain origin found in the north tower of St Mary's; it predates the fabric of the church itself.
Right: St Mary's, Bruton, Christmas Eve, 2020; considered by Nikolaus Pevsner 'the proudest church in East Somerset'. (Photo: Author)

The south door of the church served as the private entrance for the Berkeley family, owners of Bruton Abbey. It is thought members of the Berkeley family always had night-time funerals and burials. The chancel is of Georgian vintage, the earlier medieval chancel being deemed too small when it was rebuilt in 1743 by Nathaniel Ireson of Wincanton, the builder of nearby Stourhead House.

Agriculture, Trade and Industry

AGRICULTURAL PRODUCE FROM the area was brought to Bruton market, which had been established by the early twelfth century. Cattle, horses, pigs, goats and sheep were pastured all around the medieval town and crops were grown on the levelled lynchets on the hillsides. The town's open field system is recalled in the modern street names of Westfield and Eastfield.

The manufacture of woollen cloth, as in many other settlements in the West Country, was a long-established industry in Bruton. Six mills were listed in association with the royal manor in Domesday, one of which might have been the fulling mill at Combe, mentioned in a thirteenth-century source. This was still in operation in the early nineteenth century. Fullers,

Bruton from Coombe Hill, postcard dated 1902; from medieval times to the present day agriculture has been a constant in the economic life of Bruton and the countryside around.

Gants Mill; its name is derived from its original thirteenth-century owner, John le Gaunt; two mills at Pitcombe were recorded in the Domesday Book in 1086. (Photo: Gregory Beedle)

dyers, weavers and tailors appear in documents dating from the late twelfth century. Fulling mills were built at various locations along the Brue. One of these, Gants Mill in Pitcombe, has late thirteenth-century origins and is still in use. By the fourteenth century Bruton had become a prosperous wool town. Bruton was still 'much occupied' with cloth-making in the 1540s. Other craftspeople in the town in 1327 included a smith, a mason and a brewer, and there was also at least one taverner. By the start of the sixteenth century the town had a spicer, a chapman and a goldsmith. Several merchants managed the business of the buying and selling of goods in the town. Limestone was burnt in the parish in the fourteenth century – an ancient local industry that continued for centuries thereafter.

It is difficult to estimate the size of the later medieval population. The 207 households of Bruton, including ten at Redlynch, recorded for 1563, implies it can be numbered in hundreds rather than thousands. Nevertheless, the place was of considerable importance, not least as one where an annual assize court was held from 1268, a practice that continued until 1414 or later.

National Affairs

The de Montagu (Montacute) family, who held extensive lands in this part of Somerset, is recalled in the name of the village of Shepton Montague. Their ancestor from Normandy, Drogo de Montague, had joined Duke William in his triumphant conquest of England. One of his illustrious descendants was Simon, the first Lord Montagu (?1259–1316), who was buried at Bruton Priory. He served under Edward I, who visited the town in April 1278, in his campaigns in Wales and Gascony, both on land and at sea. He was also involved in Edward's war in Scotland and he might have participated in the battle of Falkirk in 1298. From 1299 until 1301, together with Richard de Brosco, he governed the mighty Corfe Castle in Dorset, and in 1309 he was granted custody of Beaumaris Castle. In 1310 he was made Admiral of Edward II's fleet and he continued to contribute his services on behalf of the Crown in campaigning against the Scots until his death.

Peter Randell has suggested that the considerable fine of £300 demanded of the Bruton Hundred in 1497 could well have been a punishment for the involvement of local people in the Cornish Rebellion in the reign of Henry VII. Described by John Guy as 'the most important revolt in Henry's reign', this rebellion was provoked by the demand for additional taxes needed to raise revenue with which to pay for a projected invasion of Scotland. Setting out from Cornwall, a raggle-taggle band of, ultimately, some 15,000 rebels made its way through Somerset towards London, gathering support as it marched, before its decisive defeat by a royal force on 17 June. In the same year one Robert Sexeye of Brewham, possibly a relation of Hugh, was heavily fined for supporting the rebellious activities of the last of the Yorkist 'pretenders', Perkin Warbeck.

3
REFORMATIONS AND REBELLIONS: BRUTON IN THE SIXTEENTH AND SEVENTEENTH CENTURIES

Population and Public Health

By 1563 Bruton is recorded as comprising 207 households, ten of which were in Redlynch. In 1630 there were around 200 families in Bruton, a further thirty at Redlynch, and twenty-two at Wyke. Bouts of plague continued to afflict Bruton long after the first devastating outbreak of bubonic plague in the late 1340s. The dramatic increase in the number of burials in the town from 38 in 1596 to 82 in 1597 corresponds with the dismal history of plague in London in the same year. Further outbreaks of plague continued well into the seventeenth century. In 1610 Sir Maurice Berkeley of Bruton Abbey, a Deputy Lieutenant of Somerset, recommended a delay in the mustering of soldiers due to its presence in the county. The Great Plague of 1665 was not confined to London, and the burial records indicate it arrived in Bruton in the spring of 1666. Twenty years later, from the early spring of 1685, the town was again afflicted by the scourge of a fever that, it was reported at the time, 'proves very mortal, and gives great apprehensions of a plague'. This was the most significant health scare since the Great Plague and, for a time, it looked as if it might be as catastrophic. On this occasion, thankfully, the fever did not bring plague in its wake but it had a devastating impact upon many communities, including, it seems, Bruton. Like the plague, it was especially severe in the summer and early autumn. It followed two years of excessive drought and hard winters; the Thames at London froze for most of the winter of 1683–84. The deleterious effect of these conditions upon public health doubtless weakened resistance to the ensuing fever. Contemporary observations suggest that this disease was a form of typhus, described at the time in bills of mortality as 'spotted fever'. In 1686 the number of burials recorded for Bruton soared from forty-five in the previous year to a grim total of eighty-seven. Fortunately, it did not linger – there were just thirty-six burials in 1687.

Influenza was another fearsome disease in early-modern England. A national outbreak in the years 1557–59, possibly wiping out as much as a twelfth of the population, seems identifiable in the record of Bruton's registers. Peter Randell's calculations suggest the average number of burials in the parish doubled in the period.

Compounding the threat of disease was the spectre of famine as society suffered the full impact of what geochronologists have dubbed 'The Little Ice Age', a significant climatic shift starting around 1500 and continuing until the mid-nineteenth century. The famine of 1557–58 increased the average number of burials in the town from an annual total of less than twenty to over a hundred. A string of failed harvests between 1594 and 1597 culminated in another as Bruton's inhabitants shared the distress felt by others nationwide in this notoriously dire late-Elizabethan decade. The allied threats of widespread starvation and popular rebellion pushed the government into the epoch-defining introduction of parish-based Poor Laws as the new century began and the Tudor Age reached its end. A slump in the woollen industry on which many Brutonians relied exacerbated further harvest failure, leading to another famine in the period 1623–1625.

Some sought a new life elsewhere. One family, the Ames, made its mark in New England, which became home to John and William Ames in 1635. Their descendants became famous as the manufacturers, until 1952, of the 'Ames Shovel', standard issue for the U.S. Army, a fine example of which can be seen in Bruton Museum. During the Interregnum (1649-1660), eight young men and

The Ames shovel in Bruton Museum. (Photo: Jackie Brooks)

two women, aged between sixteen and twenty-five, departed Bruton for the Americas in the years 1655–1659. One headed for Virginia, the others were all destined for work in Barbados under conditions stipulated in their contracts as indentured servants.

The Reformation

In the second half of the reign of Henry VIII (1509–1547), papal control over the English Church was eliminated, and many of its greatest institutions were demolished; prelates remaining loyal to the pope were executed and both the Bible and liturgy were read in English. One of the king's most important servants was a Bruton man: Sir John Fitzjames of Redlynch. Sir John (c.1470–?1538), a successful London lawyer, became, in 1519, the king's attorney-general. From his Redlynch base, he was especially active as the recorder for Bristol. Back in 1502 he was made steward of Bruton manor. He conducted the Duke of Buckingham's trial for high treason in May 1521. For a time, he served as a judge on the western circuit, hearing cases in Somerset and elsewhere in the region. He became Chief Justice of the King's Bench in 1526 and was involved in further high-profile cases including the impeachment of Cardinal Wolsey in 1529. In a letter, seemingly sent from Redlynch, to the mighty Thomas Cromwell in 1533, whose own trial he would later be involved in, he apologised for his absence from proceedings in London because of illness. Later that year, however, he rode as an honoured judge in the grand procession to Westminster celebrating the coronation of Anne Boleyn.

Misjudging the state of Fitzjames' relationship with the king, his Somerset neighbour, Richard Vowles, made a serious mistake in 1537 when he complained directly to the king regarding his Chief Justice. For doing so he was sentenced to two appearances at the pillory – one at Westminster and one at Bruton. On each occasion he was further punished by the chopping off of an ear. Fitzjames was a founder of Bruton's grammar school and is buried in the town. There is no trace of the fine monument that was said once to mark his final resting place. It is his dolphin emblem that continues to be the device used by King's School for its crest.

The Henrician Reformation can be considered the single most significant turning point in Bruton's history. The dissolution of the abbey on 1 April 1539 swept away a way of life that was centuries old. The

Angel in St Mary's bearing the Fitzjames dolphin device and emblem of King's School, Bruton. (Photo: Author)

dominance of the institution in town affairs disappeared faster than the buildings in which they resided and the socio-political dynamic of the town was changed for good. The shift in religious outlook in the locality was a more gradual process that ran the course of the turbulent reigns of Edward VI and Mary I before a moderate Protestant position was settled at the start of Elizabeth's reign. Some people in the area, including members of the Fitzjames family, who could afford the substantial recusancy fines, openly retained their Catholic faith and, no doubt, plenty more endeavoured to do so in secret.

STEPHAN BATMAN

ANOTHER OF BRUTON'S high-achieving sixteenth-century sons was the cleric and writer Stephan Batman. He was born in Bruton in around 1542, the eldest son of a Dutch *émigré* who had come to England from Zwolle in the Netherlands at the start of the decade in which his son was born. Little is known of his Bruton upbringing but the absence of any record for his having achieved a degree implies that he was educated less formally, in his home environment. It has been postulated that his knowledge of and skill in the illumination of manuscripts could indicate that he was apprenticed as a 'limner' – the term used to describe a specialist in that field. In later life he was an avid collector of medieval manuscripts, annotating and sometimes illustrating his private collection of twenty-three such works. By the time he was twenty-one he had made his way towards London, leaving Bruton, seemingly, for good. He married and raised a family, and ended up, in 1570, living in Newington, Surrey, close to the Archbishop of Canterbury's Lambeth Palace. Here, as the rector of St Mary's, he was in the service of one of its most famous and influential

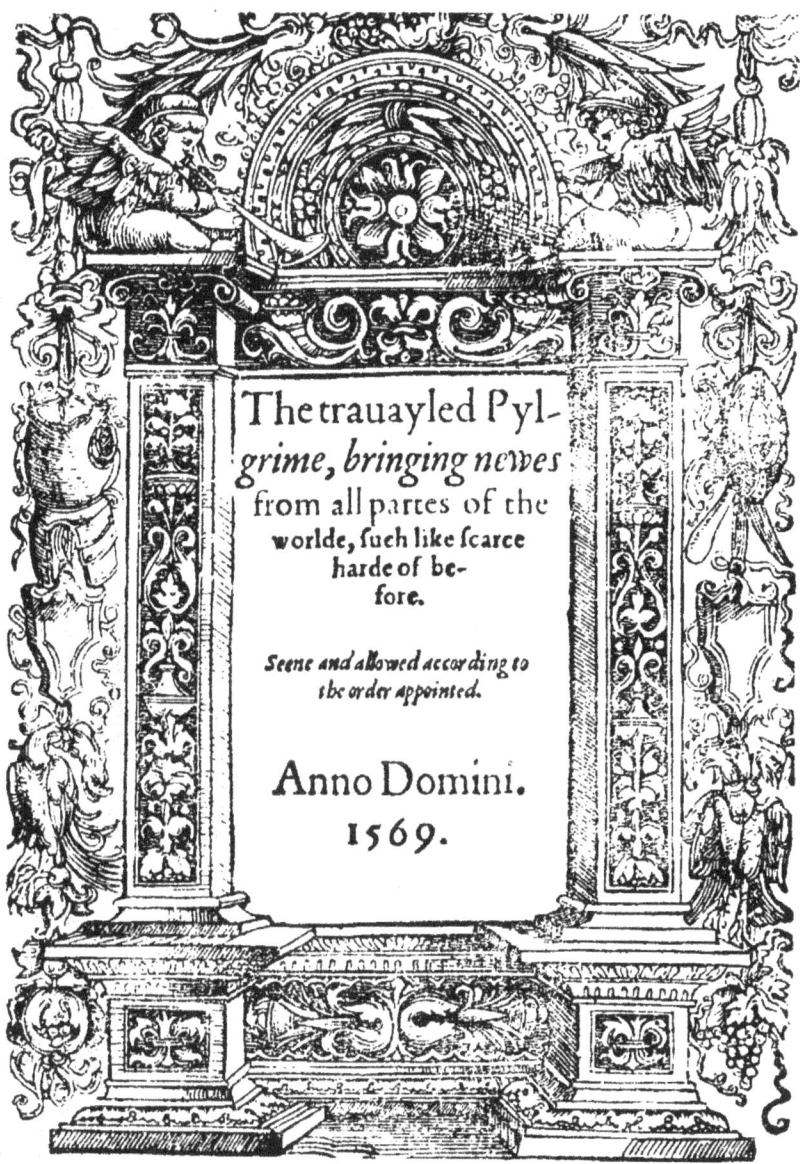

The Travayled Pylgrime (1569), *an influential work by Stephan Batman of Bruton (c.1542-1584).*

incumbents, Archbishop Matthew Parker, for whom he claimed to have acquired a vast collection of 6,700 books, the majority of which it can be presumed were printed. These, eventually, were gifted to the library of Corpus Christi College. Cambridge. Batman's father seems to have followed him from their old Bruton home for, in 1571, the Newington register recorded the burial of 'Harry Batman Father of Stephan Batman parson'. Stephan himself died early in 1584.

Batman is remembered, in particular, for *The Travayled Pylgrime* (1569), broadly in the long tradition of William Langland (*Piers Plowman*, c.1370–1390) and John Bunyan (*The Pilgrim's Progress*, 1678), but, equally, a very contemporary piece as an imaginative, allegorical and religious work comparable to Edmund Spenser's *Faerie Queene* (1590), one of the greatest expressions of the Elizabethan Renaissance. His output also included works of great scholarship, the most influential of which was *Batman upon Bartholome* (1582), containing close analyses of biblical and other ancient texts. This book was used as a source by Spenser and, probably, by William Shakespeare. Incidentally, Shakespeare's friend and the executor of his will, Thomas Russell, is believed to have been a pupil at Bruton's Free Grammar School.

The Berkeley Family

IT WAS ANOTHER loyal servant of Henry VIII, Sir Maurice Berkeley (born c.1514), gentleman usher of Henry VIII's privy chamber since 1539, who, in 1541, ended up with much of the Bruton Abbey estate in 1541. His was a junior branch of the Berkeley family of Berkeley Castle in Gloucestershire. In 1544 he was knighted and made constable of the castle. In the same year he became chief steward of the lands of Bath Abbey and he acquired the prestigious appointment as the king's chief bannerbearer in 1545. In Henry VIII's will he was bequeathed 200 marks. His signing of the device settling the crown on Lady Jane Grey in 1553 placed his career in jeopardy, yet, despite his commitment to Protestantism, he kept his head down and survived the perilous reign of 'Bloody' Mary. Under Elizabeth I his fortunes were renewed and he served as Sheriff of the counties of Somerset and Dorset in 1567 and 1568. He died in 1581.

Sir Maurice's eldest son, Henry, was an active parliamentarian and, for a time, the Keeper of Selwood Forest. In 1586 he was among those who

The Berkeley memorial in St Mary's, dating from 1580, depicts Sir Maurice, Henry VIII's, Edward VI's and Elizabeth I's standard bearer, and his two wives. (Photo: Author)

petitioned Queen Elizabeth for a speedy execution of her troublesome cousin, Mary Queen of Scots. Henry's eldest son and successor to the Bruton family seat, Maurice, bearing his grandfather's name, was returned as knight of the shire for Somerset in the year his father died. He joined the Earl of Essex's expedition to Cadiz in 1596. He died in 1617, leaving behind five sons and two daughters. The eldest son, Charles (1599–1668), took over the Bruton estate from his father and was knighted in 1622 or 1623. He married Penelope, the daughter of Sir William Godolphin, and they had at least five children – four sons and a daughter. He sat in Parliament representing a range of constituencies during the reign of Charles I and he was a deputy lieutenant for Somerset between 1625 and 1637. For a short time, he was imprisoned in London by parliamentarians at the start of the Civil War. On his release he returned to Bruton and was active in supporting the king, who visited the town on 19 July 1644. He was imprisoned again briefly, captured at Exeter when the city fell to Parliament in 1646, and again for a short time in 1651. When Charles

II was restored in 1660 he became a privy councillor and returned to parliamentary duties, spending much of his time in his London home where, among others, he entertained both the king and the famous diarist John Evelyn. However, his biographer notes, he made 'no discernible impression' on the other great diarist of the times, Samuel Pepys, and 'he appears to have been as greedy for land, money, and honours as every other Restoration courtier'. At the time of his death in 1668 he was serving as treasurer of the royal household. On 26 June that year he was buried at Bruton.

Charles' brother, William (1605–1677), historically speaking, made rather more of an impression, when he became a colonial governor. In the court of Charles I he was associated with a literary circle known as 'the Wits' and penned a number of plays. One of these, *The Lost Lady* (1638), was performed before the king and queen. He was knighted in 1639 and, in August 1641, purchased the office of governor of Virginia. He settled in Jamestown in 1642, where he built Green Spring House on land he had acquired on its western side. He became deeply involved in the export of Virginian staples – rice, spirits, flax and the like – and he was instrumental in the development of Jamestown and the westward expansion beyond Virginia's frontiers. Despite some earlier doubts regarding the direction of Charles I's policy, he remained an ardent royalist throughout the Civil War and did not hand over his government of Virginia to the English Parliament until 1652. He was restored to his former position when, at

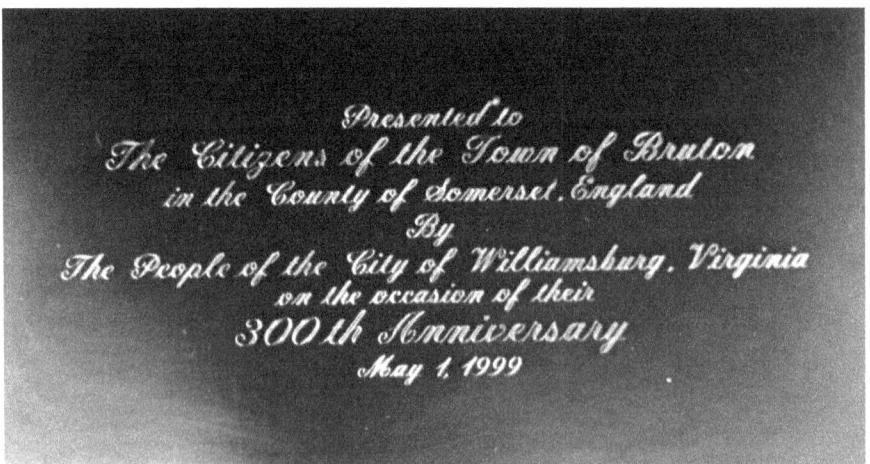

Inscription on the Williamsburg plate in Bruton Museum. (Photo: Jackie Brooks)

Bruton Parish Church, Williamsburg, Virginia. (Photo: Michael Kotrady)

the start of 1660, the year of the Restoration, the incumbent, Samuel Matthews, conveniently died. The remainder of his governorship was spent struggling to manage Virginia's and his own economic interests, and keeping control of a colony plagued by violent Native American resistance, political rivalry and a humiliating rebellion. In 1674 the new parish of Bruton, in honour of its governor, was created in Virginia where Williamsburg was subsequently established. A silver plate, now in Bruton Museum, was presented to the town to commemorate Williamsburg's 300th anniversary in 1999.

Another brother, John (c.1607–1678), who became the first Baron Berkeley of Stratton, made a name for himself as a royalist general during the English Civil War. Like his two older brothers, he both moved in courtly circles and sat in Parliament. He served the Crown as one of four generals commissioned as commander-in-chief of the king's western armies. He fought under Sir Ralph Hopton in the battle of Stratton Hill in Cornwall, a royalist victory, in 1643 and subsequently led a successful siege of Exeter. In 1645 he was made colonel-general of the king's forces in Cornwall and

Devon and he supported Lord Goring's unsuccessful siege of Taunton. His activities in the west were curtailed when the parliamentarians took back Exeter in 1646. Over the next few years he spent a good deal of time abroad and became an important member of the household of the Duke of York, the future king, James II. Following the Restoration he had various responsibilities including those of privy councillor and lord lieutenant of Ireland.

Charles Berkeley's eldest son, Maurice (1628–1690), third Viscount Fitzhardinge of Berehaven, was an MP and he held several offices in the region. He did not engage in the Civil War and, married to the stepdaughter of a parliamentary admiral, the Earl of Warwick, his career was not inhibited by the protectorate. Following the Restoration he was created, in July 1660, the first baronet of Bruton, and, in 1667, recognised as 'a great patron of mechanics', he became a fellow of the Royal Society. When the Duke of Monmouth raised rebellion against James II in 1685 he was placed in charge of the Somerset militia, which he took to confront, and defeat, Monmouth at the Battle of Sedgemoor. Nevertheless, when William of Orange marched from Devon to challenge James for the throne in 1688, he welcomed him to his seat at Bruton shortly after the first skirmish in the campaign that became known as 'the Glorious Revolution', fought at Wincanton on 20 November. Choosing not to vote against the transfer of the crown to William, he received the lieutenancy of Somerset as his reward. He died soon after, on 13 June 1690, and was buried at St Mary's.

Another son, also named Charles (c.1630–1665), became the Earl of Falmouth in 1665 after years, as a loyal Bruton Berkeley royalist, of serving in the court of the Stuarts both in exile and at home. In the service of James II both before and after he became king, he saw a good deal of action in various conflicts and was killed by cannon at sea in the battle of Lowestoft against the Dutch just three months after receiving his earldom. Despite the great affection in which he was held by the king, his biographer declares, 'He had no upstanding gifts, of intelligence, learning, or looks', and thus was not given any important political, diplomatic or administrative responsibilities. Indeed, he seems to have made himself very unpopular in certain quarters by encouraging the king's laziness and debauchery.

Falmouth's younger brother, William Berkeley, also baptised in Bruton, benefited greatly from his brother's favour at court. He was made a knight in 1664 and appointed rear-admiral of the red squadron in the 1665 campaign in which he fought alongside his brother at Lowestoft. He too was killed at sea on the first day of the Four Days' Fight against the Dutch, almost a year to the day after his brother's death at Lowestoft.

In 1698 the manor of Bruton was sold to Sir William Brownlow but bought back by William Berkeley, Baron Berkeley of Stratton, in 1717.

Bruton's Civil War

ON THE EVE of the Civil War, in the spring of 1640, the militia in Somerset were mustered to fight against the Scots. At Bruton 'all things were full of tumult' and soldiers gathered there mutinied and deserted in great numbers. In February 1643, in the second year of the war, a member of the Berkeley family and his allies raised an army of several hundred men with a view to taking both Bruton and Ilchester for the Crown. Although the details are unknown it is clear a pitched battle was fought with the people of Batcombe, long since an enclave of puritanism.

Camp crew at a re-enactment in 2019 of Bruton's fight with the Batcombites in 1643. (Photo: Author)

Meanwhile, Charles Berkeley, imprisoned in London, was commanded to instruct his tenants 'not to bear arms' against Parliament. Staunchly royalist throughout the period, and in 1644 at the height of the war, the Berkeley family had entertained Charles I, and Charles II while still Prince of Wales, in their great mansion on the Abbey site. Until 1733, the fight against the 'Batcombites' was commemorated annually with the ringing of the bells on the eve of St Matthias's Day (14 February) and it was recorded in a short verse in the pages of Bruton's register:

> All praise and thanks to God still give
> For our deliverance Matthias' Eve.
> By his great power we put to flight
> Our foes the raging Batcombites,
> Who came to plunder, burn, and slay,
> And quite consume our town this day.

The notoriously unruly, barbarous army of the royalist Lord George Goring was at large in the vicinity of Bruton in the spring of 1645. Plundering the locality for forage to feed their horses, and committing any number of unknown atrocities, they engaged with their parliamentarian enemy at various places, notably in a skirmish at Cucklington near Wincanton. The locals resisted the unwelcome presence of troops in their neighbourhoods by forming 'clubs', the 'clubmen' of which took coordinated action against any incomers, irrespective of their political affiliations, who threatened their livelihoods. In March 1646, at the end of the first Civil War, the Bruton clubmen were active again, this time protecting their communities against bands of marauding, unpaid, recently demobilised soldiers.

In the aftermath of the war there was a riot when the town was subjected to a visitation by excise commissioners. The Berkeleys however remained staunchly loyal to the Crown and hosted further royal visits, this time by James II, before he was king, in 1665, and again in 1686, shortly before he was deposed by William of Orange. Two years later, in November 1688, William and Prince George of Denmark were in the town recruiting troops. Another celebrated figure in James' reign, Thomas Ken, Bishop of Bath and Wells, preached at St Mary's on two occasions in 1687.

Bruton and the Monmouth Rebellion

In 1685 Somerset was torn apart by the Monmouth Rebellion. It was at Taunton that the Duke of Monmouth, when he arrived in the West Country in the summer of 1685, was proclaimed king by his ardent Somerset supporters. And it was in the heart of Somerset, at Sedgemoor, about twenty miles, as the crow flies, west of Bruton, that his rebellion was quashed a month later. Terrible retributions throughout Somerset came in the wake of defeat.

Following a bloody skirmish on 27 June at Norton St Philip and Monmouth's retreat to Frome, part of the royal army, led by Theophilus Oglethorpe, arrived in Bruton on its way to defeat him on Sedgemoor near Bridgwater. The battle began during the night of 5–6 July in the immediate vicinity of Westonzoyland. An estimated 300 rebels died in the field but a thousand more were killed as they fled. Just eighty or so royal troops fell. 1,500 arrests followed and Judge Jeffreys at his 'Bloody Assizes' in Taunton and elsewhere had around 250 executed; 750 or so were transported to the West Indies. Although no Bruton townsmen seem to have been arrested, some may have been involved and four were accused of supporting the rebellion. According to *A True and Exact List of the Names of all the Men that were Arraign'd and Condemn'd at Taunton in Somersetshire, in the Year 1685*, printed in

Contemporary playing card depicting the aftermath of Monmouth's failed rebellion; three of his followers were hanged in Bruton in 1689.

London in 1689, three rebels, presumably from elsewhere, were hanged here. Nearby, thirteen were listed as executed at Shepton Mallet, twelve in Frome, and six more at Wincanton. Clearly this was regarded as a region that needed teaching a lesson concerning its propensity for rebellion. Close to Bruton at Penselwood there is a lane known locally as 'Monmouth's Ride', identifying the tradition that it was part of his escape route after his defeat at Sedgemoor. Subsequently, it is said, two swords, armour and a drum dating from the period were found in the roof space, seemingly hidden, of a farm in the vicinity.

Town Life

On the eve of the Henrician Reformation the town was a prosperous place with a thriving woollen cloth industry. Other businesses included a vibrant trade in wine, imported via Bristol from France, Portugal and Spain. Maurice Berkeley was granted the town's market by the crown in 1545, which was re-granted to the family in 1565. Initially it was held at the Market Cross on Wednesdays but by the early seventeenth century Saturday was market day. Local produce sold

Weighbridge at the east end of Bruton High Street where the market cross once stood; the cross, commissioned by Abbot John Ely (1532-1539), was 18 feet tall; it was demolished in 1790 in the interests of the turnpike trust and travel by stagecoach.

there included butter and cheese, corn, fruit and meat. In his account, shortly after its construction in the 1530s, John Leland commented, 'In the market place there is a new cross of six arches, with a pillar in the centre for the market traders to stand in.' It was raised on a stepped base and sources identify a small room of some kind beneath it. Running westwards along the High Street stood rows of butchers' stalls ('shambles'). Nearby, the Town Hall was constructed in 1652 which, by 1768, was also being used as a market house. It was still standing in the 1830s. Other structures from this early modern, post-Reformation period include Quaperlake House.

In 1532 the Abbot was granted a licence for a great fair to be held on the eve, day and morrow of St George's Day (22–24 April) and another on the eve, day and morrow of the Nativity of the Virgin (7–9 September). These continued under licence when Berkeley acquired the estate. New fairs, including one in May, were permitted in the late seventeenth century. By 1617 fairs were also held in Redlynch by the Lord of the Manor.

Bruton had at least two inns in the later sixteenth century: the George and the Hart. By the start of the 1620s this had risen to six in addition to nine businesses listed as 'victuallers'. In 1686 the town's inns collectively provided beds for seventy-two guests and stabling for 142 horses. In addition to the George and the (White) Hart these seventeenth-century inns included the Green Dragon, the Unicorn, the Swan, the Three Goats' Heads, the Bull's Head, and the King's Arms.

The Poor

SINCE THE PASSING of the Elizabethan Poor Laws, the legislation concluded in 1601, the poor assembled at the north porch of St Mary's each Sunday to receive payment after evening prayers. By 1700 they suffered the further humiliation of being 'badged'– the compulsory wearing of a badge sewn on to their clothing, advertising their pauperism whilst ensuring hand-outs went to genuine claimants. By the mid-seventeenth century the parish was administered by the minister, two churchwardens, two overseers of the poor, and two constables (one who operated solely in the town, the other working elsewhere in the hundred). Later in the century the number of overseers of the poor was increased to four. They were responsible for providing Bruton's most needy inhabitants with money and clothing, and covering rents and hospital fees. Some were provided with accommodation.

Bruton had a hospital of some kind back in 1291. Towards the end of the fourteenth century a St Catherine's hospital at Lusty cared for the poor and sick, including those suffering with leprosy. From 1621 it was supported by the trustees of Hugh Sexey's gift to the town and was still extant in 1672, by which time it was an almshouse for men and boys. It seems to have been converted into a number of separate dwellings by 1717.

For those who fell foul of the law, corporal and capital punishment were the order of the day. Whippings were relatively commonplace throughout the period, the regular practice being to walk the offender, stripped to the waist and tied to the cart, for a prolonged, public, bloody whipping all the way from the Market Cross to West End. Public humiliations, for what seem from a modern perspective petty offences, included time spent in the town's stocks or pillory, both of which probably stood close to the cross.

Swanton House, the supposed home at West End of Bruton's great benefactor, Hugh Sexey. (Photo: Author)

Hugh Sexey

Hugh Sexey's bust in the quadrangle of the almshouse; it bears a coat of arms derived from the seemingly unrelated Saxey family of Bristol. (Photo: Author)

A PROPERTY AT THE west end of the High Street, Swanton House (No.91), is said to have been the home of Bruton's greatest benefactor, Hugh Sexey, who was probably born around 1540 and died in 1619. A William Sexey buried in Bruton on 15 January 1567 may have been his father and the family can be traced in the parish records back to the early fifteenth century. His bust, erected at the end of the seventeenth century, overlooks the attractive quadrangle of Sexey's Hospital, carved, many years after Sexey's death, by William Stanton of Holborn. Sexey, so the somewhat unlikely story goes, was a humble stable-lad at one of the town's inns, or possibly a shepherd (a row of sheep's heads is carved beneath the image of Sexey), who, clearly with a decent education, probably gained at the grammar school, managed to become a very successful and wealthy lawyer, directly serving the Crown.

By 1566 Sexey was working as an attorney in London and living at Redcross Street in Cripplegate. He acquired leases on Crown properties in South Molton, Devon, and elsewhere in Somerset, Wiltshire and Gloucestershire, some for his own benefit and some on behalf of wealthy families including the Berkeleys. His lucrative appointments included localised roles as steward, bailiff, auditor, and collector of rents on behalf of, among others, the Crown and the Bishop of Bath and Wells.

He married twice but was not survived by any children and his fortune was bequeathed to the town. Even before his death he seems to have acquired a reputation for benevolence, having converted a number of small houses in Bruton into suitable homes for the poor of the town who were also granted 'certain small weekly maintenance'. These included

Sexey's Hospital and gardens viewed from Lower Backway. (Photo: Author)

six houses on the north side of the High Street, opposite the site of what would become Sexey's Hospital, which subsequently became known as the Old Almshouse before they were demolished in 1876–77 to make way for a garden for Old Brewery House over the road. He died in London on 19 August 1619.

The original wing of the fine almshouse paid for by the fortune Sexey bequeathed, and which takes his name, was not completed until 1632. The beautiful woodwork in the chapel, in which the Master of the Hospital conducted services twice daily, dates from the seventeenth century.

The 'Armada Chest' or 'Treasure Chest', still in the main hall at Sexey's Hospital, is the chest identified in the deed of incorporation, prescribing rules for the hospital, drawn up in 1638. This placed the supervision of the almshouse in the hands of 'Twelve Visitors' who oversaw the work of the 'Corporation' that comprised the Master, eight governors, and twelve 'poor aged persons'. The title deeds were to be placed in the chest which has six locks opened by a set of six keys, one held by each pair of Visitors, thus safeguarding them from tampering by the Corporation.

Sexey's Hospital has a long history of keeping a well-maintained fruit, flower and vegetable garden. The gardens have always been a special and much admired feature of the Hospital. Records show that in 1814 each inmate would have a plot of the garden, as well as a room with a

REFORMATIONS AND REBELLIONS

An old postcard showing the interior of the chapel at Sexey's Hospital.

The witches of Selwood Forest; Joseph Glanvill, Sadicusmus Triumphatus (1681), frontispiece (hand-tinted detail).

bed and blanket, a blue coat or gown with red initials to wear, coal to burn in winter, and a weekly allowance of six shillings. In addition to the educational foundations set up in Sexey's name in Bruton, a school was also established on his estate at Blackford near Wedmore, now the Hugh Sexey Church of England Middle School.

THE WITCHES OF BREWHAM

ANYONE WITH A passing interest in English witchcraft belief will be familiar with Lancashire's Pendle Forest witch-hunts but few, even among those who live here, are aware of the equally rich witchcraft history of Selwood Forest and the seventeenth-century covens found in Brewham and nearby Stoke Trister.

Between 1613 and 1642, during the reigns of James I and Charles I, Richard Bernard, a puritan and prolific writer of theological and other texts, was the rector of Batcombe, close to Bruton. Using the evidence of numerous confessions of witches, he constructed an up-to-date mythology of witchcraft and diabolism. *A Guide to Grand-Jury Men in Cases of Witchcraft*, published in 1627, was widely read, not least by the notorious mid-1640s witch-hunter in the Home Counties, Matthew Hopkins, the self-styled 'Witchfinder-General', and those involved in the notorious Salem witch trials in America. Dedicated to the judges of the Western Circuit, Bernard's *Guide to Grand Jury Men* ultimately defined the legal and metaphysical position of witch-finders in England and the colonies in the seventeenth century. Bernard's views were further dispersed through their incorporation in the third edition (1630) of Michael Dalton's highly influential *Country Justice*, first published in 1618.

The Brewham witchcraft cases, recorded by a local magistrate, Robert Hunt of Compton Pauncefoot, were first published by Joseph Glanvill, a member of the Royal Society and Vicar of Frome. His monumental *Saducismus Triumphatus, Concerning Witches and Apparitions* appeared in 1681. Hunt supplied Glanvill with five 'relations' concerning the activities of numerous witches close to Bruton. These included accounts of feasting, dancing, and the ritual baptising of wax effigies at 'black sabbath' meetings convened by the Devil who, in the guise of a handsome man in black, led the proceedings. These coincided with the passing of the first Conventicle Act in 1664 that forbade meetings for religious worship, other than in family prayer, outside of the Church. It is possible that the mysterious men in black in the accounts were puritan ministers dismissed from their posts at the time of the Restoration. Of particular interest in this context is Edward Bennett, born in South Brewham in 1618. After serving as curate to Richard Bernard, the demonologist of Batcombe, he held a living in Dorset from which he was removed in 1662. Having returned to his birthplace he spent a couple of months in Ilchester gaol in 1665, the year in which the Brewham witches were tried. In 1672, new legislation for religious toleration was passed and he, among several other Bruton ministers, was licensed to use his home as a Presbyterian meeting house. It can be concluded there had been several illicit conventicles in the area in the preceding years.

Christian Green (alias Cornish) of Brewham claimed she first met the Devil at 'Mr Hussey's Ground in Brewham Forest'. She and her associates confessed to further diabolical meetings at Brewham Common and Redmore, an extra-parochial district of Brewham in the vicinity of Brewham Lodge, below the source of the Brue. At Hussey's Knap, Green made her covenant with the Devil, 'in the shape of a man in blackish clothes', having been persuaded that in so doing she might evade her present state of acute poverty. After giving her 'four-pence-half-penny', with which she bought bread in Brewham, he vanished 'leaving a smell of brimstone behind'. Her familiar, the imp by which she caused magical harm, took the form of a hedgehog.

Green was the first of six Brewham people examined by Hunt between March and June 1665. Those with her 'in covenant with the Devil' – her coven – included two more Brewham women, Catharine Green and Margaret Agar, and, 'three or four times', Mary Warberton, also of Brewham. 'That rampant hag' Agar's supposed crimes are the main focus of these testimonies:

> Margaret Agar brought [...] an image in wax for Elizabeth, the wife of Andrew Cornish of Brewham, and the Devil in the shape of a man in black clothes baptized it and then stuck a thorn into its head. Agar stuck one into its stomach, and Catharine Green one into its side. She further says that, prior to this, Agar said she would hurt Elizabeth Cornish, who since the baptizing of the image has been very ill.

The Church of St John the Baptist, Brewham. (Derek Rayner, 1999)

She was accused of killing her neighbours' cattle and bewitching to death Joseph Talbot, the Overseer of the Poor, who 'made her children go to service and refused to give them such good clothes as she desired'. Elizabeth Talbot described the suddenness of her father's illness and its severity, 'as if he had been stabbed with daggers'. After four or five days he was dead. Agar was sent to prison some time before 3 June 1665, but she survived the ordeal and was buried in the parish in October 1670.

Another local woman, Mary Green, also confessed to her involvement in night-time sabbats, and she listed several more participants: Alice Green, Dinah and Dorothy Warberton, Joan Syms, Margaret Clark, and Henry Walter. The little man in black she described as wearing a hat, speaking 'low but big', and answering to the name Robin. The names of most of these characters can be found in the parish records which also include the burial record of one of their supposed victims, Richard Greene (alias Cornish), who was buried in the village at the end of April 1663. There is clear evidence in the case of the close and familial relationship between the accused, their accusers and their alleged victims. Whatever else was going on there can be no doubt that this was the product of vicious, internecine feuds in a remote rural community, some of those involved living on the margin, hopelessly dependent on their neighbours.

Between 23 January and 15 March 1665, Hunt, the JP, heard the statements of at least thirteen people across thirteen days of investigation. More than twenty people, some men but mostly women, were recorded as attending the sabbats at various places in the vicinity of Bruton and Wincanton. Glanvill deeply regretted the ending of Hunt's pursuit of witches in the area: 'Had not his discoveries and endeavours met with great opposition and discouragement from some then in authority', he wrote, 'the whole clan of those hellish confederates in these parts might have been justly exposed and punished.'

Bruton's Seventeenth-Century Witchcraft Trial

In the winter of 1689/90, four years after what is thought to have been the last execution for witchcraft in England – that of Alice Molland in Exeter in 1685 – a remarkable case of witchcraft was heard at Bruton's new court-house, built in 1684, on the north side of the High Street. Here local magistrates heard allegations brought against some elderly women who lived in Beckington, near Frome.

The earliest account of these events appeared in a double-side broadsheet, printed in London in 1689 under the heading *Great News from the West of England*. In 1691, in his book *The Certainty of the Worlds of Spirits*, an influential puritan minister, Richard Baxter, included another version of the case, sent to him by Beckington's rector. The survival of two distinct records of the same episode makes for an exceptionally rich account.

The tale begins with the activities of a lad from a poor family, William Spicer, who, 'as he was wont to pass by the Alms-house (where lived an Old Woman, about Four-score) he would call her *Witch*, and tell her off her *Buns*', by which he meant her demon-familiars. In revenge, the woman 'threatened him with a *Warrant*, and accordingly did fetch one from a Neighbouring *Justice of the Peace*, at which he was so frightened, that he humbled himself to her, and promised never to call her so again'. Nevertheless, 'Within a few days after this the Young Man fell into the strangest Fits that ever Mortal beheld with Eyes.' He began to suffer with fits, visions, and bouts of vomiting pins, a curious but prevalent feature of many English witchcraft narratives by this time: 'when he did call for some *Small Beer* to drink, he would be sure to bring up some *Crooked Pins*; first and last, to the Number of Thirty, and upwards'. William Spicer's record of baptism has survived and is dated 28 August 1670: the author of *Great News* was absolutely correct in suggesting he was around eighteen years old at the time of his supposed bewitchment.

Another eighteen-year-old, Mary Hill, baptised at Beckington in April 1671, also made an enemy of the old woman, first in a dispute over possession of a ring, next because she refused to accompany her to find spinning work in neighbouring Frome, and, finally, because she denied her the gift of an apple. Mary soon became ill with the same afflictions as William. Her strange vomiting was spectacular, throwing up threaded needles, nails over three inches long, brass spoon handles, and large lumps of lead and iron. This sort of evidence, presented in physical form before the judges, fabricated or otherwise, might have been enough to sway opinion.

Horned demon in Bruton Museum (c. mid-twelfth century) found in the basement of 17 Quaperlake Street, possibly originating from Bruton Priory. (Photo: Author)

The octogenarian accused of Mary's bewitchment was one Elizabeth Carrier and they were closely acquainted. Just as the 'witch' conformed to stereotype, so did the bewitched – young and troubled, a recently orphaned teenage girl living off the parish with younger siblings to support. Close scrutiny of the parish records reveals Carrier had the task of laying out the dead in the village and she had been especially busy at the time of a severe typhus epidemic a couple of years before. It is reasonable to suppose she had long attended the living as well as the dead, perhaps as a midwife or as a healer – one of the so-called 'cunning folk' who provided remedies, magical ones perhaps, for her neighbours.

With the whole community rising up against her, Carrier was subjected to three 'swimmings' in the River Frome. This horrible ordeal

Bruton's court house on the north side of High Street, opened in 1684, in which evidence against the Beckington witches was heard in the winter of 1689/90. (Photo: Author)

was not considered part of the due process of English law and hence, we can assume, most cases of its application were not recorded. Records of at least twenty-six cases of witch-swimming in England survive for the period 1612 to 1795, the majority of which post-date the 1660s. In the 1689 tract her ordeal was described in considerable detail: 'her Legs being tied, she was put in, and tho' she did endeavour to the uttermost (by her Hands), to get herself under, yet she could not, but would lie upon her Back, and did Swim like a piece of Cork'. To prove her guilt 'there was put into the Water, a Lusty young Woman, who sunk immediately, and had been drown'd, had it not been for the help that was at hand'. Most of the people watching, 200 or more, including many 'Persons of Quality', were convinced. One 'person of quality' who visited the village *incognito* to investigate the case was William Player of Castle Cary who had recently built for himself a fine new home at Hadspen that evolved into Hadspen House, now the fine hotel at the centre of The Newt in Somerset estate, three miles south of Bruton.

Having survived her swimmings, orders were given to have Carrier searched for 'Marks and Tokens of a Witch' and she was committed to the county gaol at Ilchester. Soon afterwards charges were brought against Ann More and Margery Coombes, her alleged accomplices, and, following their hearing at the Bruton sessions, they too were sent to Ilchester to await trial at the next Western Circuit assizes. Before the case was heard, and thrown out, by Justice Holt at Taunton in April 1690, Coombes died in the notoriously unhealthy confines of Ilchester Gaol – another forgotten victim in the later history of England's witch-hunts.

Bruton's Early Quaker Community

A FEW YEARS BEFORE, in 1684, a case of what many at the time considered another version of witchcraft – Quakerism – was being heard at Bruton. Quakers were resident in Bruton from at least 1661. Over ninety Quaker 'Friends' were made to appear at the 1684 sessions. In the words of a petition they presented to the bench at the start of the proceedings, they were being treated as 'Criminals, charged for the Breach of our Duty to God and the King', accused of 'Riotous Assemblies' and 'Seditious Conventicles', and 'our not conforming to those Worships that we have no Faith in'. This trial had a happier outcome than Elizabeth Carrier's in 1689 for Lord Fitzharding and his deputy judge, Sir Edward Phillips, 'being pretty Moderate', set most of them free. They appeared before the magistrates over many days in their neighbourhood groups –

Chew Magna, Glastonbury, Stoke St Gregory, Ilminster, Wiveliscombe, Shepton Mallet, Long Sutton. In all eighty-three Friends were discharged and only seven or eight returned to the County Gaol at Ilchester. It was said at the time that Phillips, who seems to have taken the principal judicial role in the proceedings, was running for Parliament; the release of Quakers – many of whom were successful tradesmen and significant local employers, and whose employees faced starvation so long as their masters remained in prison – was an astute political gesture. The unprecedented clampdown on peaceful non-conformists, which had vastly over-stretched the county's very limited capacity for incarceration, had been addressed by moderation and good sense. The persecution of Bruton's Quaker community was much diminished as a consequence of the Toleration Act in 1689. One of its leading lights was Thomas Whitehead, formerly of North Cadbury, who was a principal employer as an important Bruton clothier. He had endured terms in prison and many fines for his beliefs in the years before his death in 1691. Nevertheless, he died a very wealthy man, his personal and household goods valued at over £6,806. In the mid-eighteenth century Bruton's Quakers appear to have used the Market Hall/Courtroom building, where the Beckington witchcraft case was heard, as its meeting place.

4
POVERTY AND PLENTY: BRUTON IN THE EIGHTEENTH AND NINETEENTH CENTURIES

Population and Public Health

Between the late eighteenth century and the mid-nineteenth the population of Bruton doubled. When Collinson was compiling his history of Somerset for publication in 1791, he found 'The average number of christenings in this parish is 56, of burials 66.' In the relatively densely populated parish of South Brewham there were around twenty-five annual christenings and seventeen burials among a population living in about eighty houses, many in Hardway. Another sixty or so houses were in North Brewham. In Bruton there were around 320 houses in the town, and 1,600 inhabitants. Wyke Champflower, 'well-wooded, and surrounded by hills finely cultivated', had fifteen. Pitcombe had forty houses, including some in the hamlets of Hadspen and Cole. Upton Noble had thirty-six whereas Redlynch had a mere eight. Collinson commented on the 'exceedingly pleasant' location of Milton Clevedon on the north slope of Creech Hill, 'with a fine rich vale beneath it, and Smallcombe hill in front'. Then, as now, its thirty-six or so houses were mostly along the main road. Yarlington, occupying another 'pleasant vale, surrounded by small hills, and divided into fine and well-cultivated inclosures', had forty-six houses, the majority on the village street near the church.

The first census in 1801 recorded a population for the town of 1,631, rising to 2,223 by 1831. It stayed around this number for the next few decades but, by 1891, it had reduced to 1,776. Bruton's poorer folk lived in overcrowded, squalid homes – tiny cottages in the courtyards and bartons at West End and running along the High Street.

Over the course of the seventeenth and early eighteenth centuries smallpox became a more common cause of death in England as epidemics spread across the country. When smallpox inoculation was still a recent development and, in any case, a dangerous practice, and before the miracle of vaccination was proclaimed by Dr Jenner in the 1790s, it was a lethal and terrifying disease. It was in the town in 1674 and 1675, and 1737 was a particularly bad year for the town when 443 of its inhabitants were found to be infected, of whom 34 died as a consequence. From 1764 the parish provided the services of a surgeon and an apothecary who administered inoculations. In 1853 vaccinations became compulsory by Act of Parliament.

Although the average age of death in Bruton rose steadily from 34.4 in 1854 to 53.3 in 1894, public health reports for Bruton in the 1870s painted a picture of urban deprivation, overcrowding, contamination of water supplies, and filth. In such conditions typhoid, dysentery, diarrhoea, bronchitis, pneumonia and pleurisy were rife. From 1769, the parish overseers of the poor had appointed a 'scavenger' to clear the streets. Those found responsible for the dung-heaps in the town's bartons and backways were liable to fines. It was a typhoid outbreak in 1871 that prompted the headmaster of King's, A.D. Gill, to write to the Sanitary Commissioners regarding sewage in the mill stream in Lower Backway, a situation exacerbated by the keeping of pigs in backyards and the presence of the town centre's two abattoirs. The subsequent report was grim, its findings including polluted wells, a scarcity of toilets, and human excrement discovered in 'nearly every alley and byeway of the Town'. The Brue itself was, effectively, the town's drain. In 1872 the offensive mill stream was covered over and an important but polluted communal well, Patwell, acquired its pump-house, but it would be several decades before significant improvements were made.

Patwell pump-house. (Photo: Author)

The River Brue into which effluent was emptied from 'necessary houses' along its banks, the discharge pipe of this one beside the stepping-stones is obscured by summer foliage. (Photo: Author)

In 1734 a workhouse was established on Silver Street in buildings between Church Bridge and Bow Bridge. Here the poor were engaged in spinning and knitting. Between 1735 and 1835 the number of workhouse residents fluctuated, peaking at an average of thirty-eight in 1755 but not exceeding twenty in the period 1802–1835. In the garden between the workhouse and the river its inmates grew vegetables. Here too, thatched like many other buildings in the town, was the 'Necessary House', its effluent no doubt discharged directly into the Brue. Close by once stood the parish roundhouse (lock-up) which, together with the workhouse, was maintained by the Overseers of the Poor. With the passing of the Poor Law Amendment Act in 1834 and the creation of the new Union Workhouse at Wincanton, half of the Bruton workhouse premises were sold off to the trustees of the Sunday School in 1836. The school was rebuilt in 1856 when the modern car park area became its playground.

Another view of the once polluted Brue running through the heart of the town; note what appears to be another 'necessary house' on the left bank. Today the river runs clear under Bow Bridge where children paddle and catch fish in their nets, but as late as the mid-twentieth century it was said to be 'garbage-soiled'.

Hard Times

FOOD RIOTS OCCURRED in England in many places and on many occasions throughout the eighteenth century. The closing decade of the century was marked by some of the most threatening of these localised insurrections. 1795 and 1800–01 were years of severe dearth as supply and demand issues in the context of the wars against Napoleon caused a surge in food prices. A popular protest against the price of foodstuff in Bruton's market-place on 2 May 1795 necessitated the calling of the Castle Cary mounted yeomanry before it was dispersed. Two millers on their way home from the Saturday market in Bruton in 1800 were lucky to escape injury when someone fired a blunderbuss at them.

The so-called 'allotment movement' starting in around 1793, at the start of the Napoleonic Wars, was driven by the need to alleviate declining rural living standards. The crisis of the agricultural riots that spread westwards from the south-east of England in 1830 contributed to the formation of the Labourer's Friend Society in the same year. The LFS took the lead in the allotment campaign over the next two decades, revival of interest in which was probably almost entirely due to the shock of destruction of property and threat of violence by ordinary folk protesting under the banner of an imagined leader, Captain Swing, in much the same way as a couple of decades before machine-breakers in the north of the country, nicknamed 'Luddites', had created the pretence of being organised and led by one General Ludd. Following harvest failure in 1829, the Swing movement started in Kent in June 1830 and rapidly spread north into East Anglia and westwards across the southern counties. Hay-ricks and barns were set alight and the new labour-saving threshing machines were a particular target of this new breed of rural Luddite. By the end of the year Swing protests had arrived in Somerset. *The Times* reported the activities of 'a mob of several hundred persons' at Henstridge, just twelve miles south of Bruton, which had destroyed local farmers' machines. On 26 November 1830 a barn and stable were burned to the ground in South Brewham, and two days later Sir Richard Colt Hoare witnessed a great mob of hungry, bludgeon-bearing protesters pass his Stourhead home. He urged his tenants to stop using threshing machines until calm was restored. Troops were mustered briefly in local towns, including Bruton, and hundreds of special constables were sworn in at Wincanton before Swing's westward march finally petered out in the following year.

From 1830 the Bishop of Bath and Wells led the allotment campaign in Somerset and it is unlikely to be a coincidence that Bruton's local

Tumble-down cottages at the southern end of Church Bridge; the town workhouse adjoined them to the right of this old photograph.

champion thereafter was a Brewham man – Captain Scobell – who praised allotments for keeping labourers 'from idleness, or worse than idleness'. By 1832 Bruton's Overseers of the Poor had a scheme in place for the rental of small plots of land for local people to grow potatoes. Bruton's major employer of silk-workers, J.S. Ward, chaired the first meeting of the Bruton Field Garden Society in December 1840. In his inaugural address he remarked on the benefit to over 130 tenants of allotments on land gifted to the town by the Earl of Ilchester and Sir Henry Hoare. One plot of land commanded by the society was on Dropping Lane, probably at the same location as the present allotments provided for community use in more recent times by Hauser & Wirth of Durslade Farm, another major employer and generous benefactor of the town.

Further food riots occurred in several market towns in the region, including Bruton, in November 1867. This seems to have been well organised, ceremonial and peaceable, entailing a procession and a marching band. Participants, 'mostly females' according to one report, shouted 'Down with the bread!' and other slogans, abused a few local tradesmen and smashed a few windows as they paraded through the town.

Work

AGRICULTURE REMAINED THE main business in and around early modern Bruton. By the end of the nineteenth century horse-powered machinery such as the horse rake and hay-cutting machine had arrived on Bruton's farms. The railway brought with it an unprecedented demand for dairy produce. In 1818, towards the end of the reign of 'Farmer' George III, in an age of enthusiasm for agricultural improvement and following in the footsteps of the pioneering Bath and West Agricultural Society (established 1777), Bruton's Agricultural Society was founded and the town's first annual 'Cattle Show' was held. By 1891 it had evolved into the East Somerset Agricultural Society, having joined forces with the Wincanton and Castle Cary societies.

At the start of the seventeenth century Bruton's tradesmen included tailors, maltsters, scriveners, tallow chandlers and glaziers. Metalworkers in the town included, by the late seventeenth century, a cutler, and a highly skilled goldsmith, Gabriel Felling. Felling was trained in London and lived in Bruton by 1678, where he died in 1714. A flagon by Felling was acquired by St Mary's Church in 1706 and a fine Felling tankard was bought by Bruton Museum in 2017. His work can also be seen in the Museum of Somerset, Taunton, and the Victoria & Albert Museum, London. At least two traders were issuing their own tokens. The production of cloth, serges and broadcloth, remained the main business of the town's craftspeople. Prosperous clothiers included Thomas Whitehead (d. 1691), a first-generation Quaker. By 1717 the town was specialising in fine Spanish medleys and also the production of stockings. In 1742 it still enjoyed, according to Stuckey, 'a great trade in serges and stockings'. There was also some weaving of flax by the 1750s. One of the town's mills, located at West End, had been converted to

The Felling tankard in Bruton Museum. (Photo: Dave Watts)

grinding-edged tools by the middle of the century. It had ceased to be a blade mill by 1768 and probably became a silk mill.

In the late eighteenth century woollen cloth production gave way to silk when George Ward established a silk-throwing mill in the town in 1769. Fairly soon 300–400, mostly young, local people were engaged in silk reeling at factories owned by the family including one, presumed to have been established in the medieval period, opposite their Glen House home in Quaperlake Street. The Wards also had interests in silk mills in Evercreech and Over Stowey. Silk Mill Lane, running off High Street at its western end, denotes the small factory that in 1816 employed eighteen women and children, and two male overlookers. In that year, John Sharrer Ward was employing 1,000 workers, a third below the age of eighteen, in just two mills. In 1821 more than half the families in the parish were engaged in either manufacture or trade and, despite the business of three silk mills, the main activity was the making of stockings. In 1833 John & Samuel Saxon employed 300 hands in their mills, including sixty female apprentices, contracted for seven years from the age of nine. The silk industry in the town was in decline by the early 1830s and by around 1850 the focus of the silk industry had shifted north to Macclesfield. At the

West End; the building with the arched window jutting into the road on the left is Town Mill House which had a water wheel in place until 1970; the base of the gas lamp on the right can still be seen embedded in the wall.

start of the last decade of the eighteenth century Collinson reported, 'The only manufacture is a little hosiery, and silk reeling, at the latter of which between three and four hundred young persons are generally employed.' In 1841 J.S. Ward still had two silk factories, and the Saxons had one operating at West End but a second factory there had already closed. Gants Mill, having operated as a fulling mill for centuries, was a silk mill from 1810 until 1840.

Throughout the period some of the mills retained served agricultural purposes, grinding wheat, flour and malt. In 1819 there were two flour mills – one at West End, the other at Combe. Other activities in the parish included quarrying on the east side of Dropping Lane and lime-burning. In the nineteenth century there were five lime-kilns in operation at quarry sites. The surviving back wall and ramp of a kiln and its neighbouring quarry were recorded at Cuckoo Hill in 1998. Good examples can also be found in Upton Noble.

For many Brutonians the working day was very long – even as the nineteenth century gave way to the twentieth, twelve- or thirteen-hour days were not unusual. Of child labour in the late 1860s it was reported that 'Boys go out very early to work, some at 6 or 7 years old; they drive plough, keep birds, pick apples &c. They must work because wages are so low.' Children in 1833 routinely worked in J.S. Ward's silk mills for some time before they reached the age of nine because, as he said at the time, 'we must take them on at an earlier period in order to make them useful'.

The wealth of eighteenth- and nineteenth-century Bruton is evident in the considerable number of fine houses erected in that period, notably along Quaperlake Street. Away from the built-up centre several grand detached homes were built, such as Marksdanes, Cliff House, Berkeley House, Tolbury House, and Whaddon House. Such dwellings housed servants as well as family members. By 1861, according to the evidence of that year's census, sixty Bruton families had one or more domestic servants. Most were female.

By the mid-seventeenth century Bruton had a well-established community of professionals including apothecaries, attorneys, clockmakers, physicians and surgeons. Quaperlake Street's fine houses support the claim that this is where Bruton's gentlemen lived. The Quaperlake mill subsequently became a horsehair factory in the middle of the nineteenth century where, until 1883, around 100 people at any one

Quaperlake Street, a name probably derived from 'quabb', Old English for a marsh. (Mid-twentieth-century postcard)

time prepared horsehair for the padding of seats. In 1900 it became the site of the Bruton bacon factory. For a time Quaperlake Street also had an iron foundry, specialising in frames for power looms used in the north of England cotton industry.

'This is a good market-town,' declared Collinson in 1791. At the start of the eighteenth century, Bruton held two fairs attracting dealers in horses, cattle and pigs. Stuckey's *Compleat History of Somersetshire*, published in 1742, mentioned Bruton's weekly market on Saturdays and an annual fair each St George's Day (23 April). In 1821 markets were held twice – 21 April and 9 September – in the tradition of the annual medieval spring and autumn markets held around St George's Day and the Nativity of the Virgin. The September gathering was known as the 'Bruton Veast'. Although the town is recorded as having had a cattle show in early December in 1835, and one after the second Thursday every October by 1883, *Kelly's Directory* for 1897 identifies annual fairs for cattle still being held, in the ancient tradition, in April and September. In the 1920s they moved to a yard in Patwell Lane before coming to an end in 1936. On Market Day the pubs, which usually ended their lunchtime trade at 2 pm, were permitted to stay open until 4 pm.

The first Bruton Co-operative shop opened in Bruton in 1902. Membership of the Co-op played an important part in the economic and

POVERTY AND PLENTY

Cattle Market, early twentieth century; this is now the site of the industrial estate on Station Road.

The Co-operative stores on Patwell Street in c. 1953. Bruton's Co-op opened in 1901, took over the bacon factory on Quaperlake Street and had its own slaughterhouse. It also had its own creamery and its business extended to branches in Evercreech, Wincanton, and Castle Cary.

social lives of many families. From 1918, it held its annual Gala Day, starting with a procession led by the town band and followed by a fair, prize-giving and dancing in Jubilee Park. The Co-op continued to provide for the community until the 1960s.

At the start of the nineteenth century a forlorn attempt was made to find coal on the eastern side of South Brewham. A company was formed, shares were sold and several shafts were dug, one to a depth of 200 metres. No coal was found and in 1810, after six years of prospecting, the enterprise was wound up.

Communications

THE STATE OF roads around Bruton before the turnpike revolution associated with the eighteenth century was amply summed up by the intrepid traveller Celia Fiennes, who passed this way in, or shortly before, 1687. Fiennes (1662–1741) lived at Newton Toney, near Salisbury, and began journeying around England 'to regain my health by variety and change of aire and exercise' – her long life being proof of her premise. Following a visit to Stonehenge, 'that is reckon'd one of the wonders of England', she went directly to Yeovil, then on to Mere, where she saw the excavation of stone remains on its grassed castle mound; from there to Wincanton 'which is on a steep hill and very stony; you go down through the town all the way down as it were a steep precipice, all rocks'. From Wincanton she visited the 'good fruitfull country' around Castle Cary and travelled the two miles to Alford, famed locally for the quality of 'minerall water which Company resorts to for drinking' and which was sought after for brewing beer. The local country folk, alas, proved 'a clounish rude people'. From there she went to Bruton, 'a very neate stone built town'. Returning home, presumably following the path of what became the A303, she faced the challenge of Dropping Hill before she could leave Bruton behind:

> from it we ascend a very high steep hill all in a narrow lane cut out of the rocks, and the way is all like stone steps; the sides are rocks on which grow trees thick, their roots run amongst the rocks, and in many places fine cleare springs buble out, and run a long out of the rocks, it smells just like the sea; we were full an hour passing that hill, though with four horses and a Chariot, my Sister self and maid.

Despite expensive repairs to it in 1762–63, the passage for wheeled traffic on the bridge was tight because, like other bridges in the vicinity, notably Frome's principal river bridge, it had houses built along it – three houses and at least two 'tenements' are recorded being there in the early eighteenth century. There were still two houses on the bridge as late as 1819.

A toll house to the east of the town; an equally fine example is on Shute Lane at West End. (Photo: Author)

Bruton's turnpike trust was established by Act of Parliament by 1756 and wound up in 1876. Inevitably there was a measure of opposition to the imposition of tolls which probably accounted, in part, for the local episodes of tollhouse-related crime. In 1840, for example, three men were fined for assaulting a Redlynch tollgate keeper and, back in 1786, a gun was fired into the window of a tollhouse on Creech Hill.

By the 1790s Bruton had five waggons taking goods to and from London and by 1840 there was a regular coach service from Bruton to Bath and Weymouth. Trade directories from the period identify the emergence of shops and shopkeepers, including one specialising in toys. In the mid-

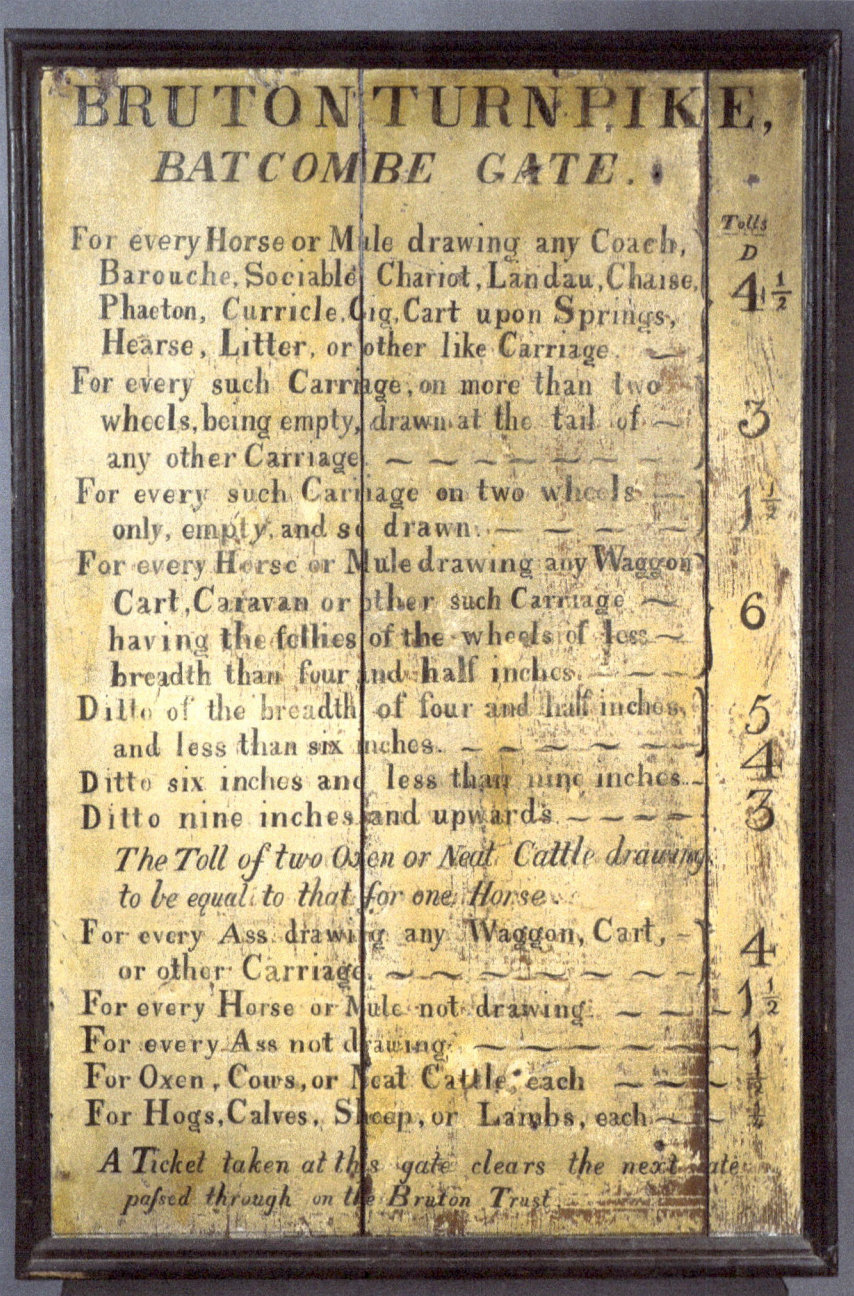

Bruton Turnpike Trust toll-board in Bruton Museum. (Photo: Dave Watts)

nineteenth century Bruton's professional class included a bank manager, an auctioneer, two solicitors and a printer. New businesses included two breweries and, by 1883, two timber merchants.

Bruton's railway, providing a connection to London, arrived in 1856. A contemporary report recorded the opening of the 25 ¾ miles between Frome and Yeovil and the related celebrations at Bruton held on 3 September 1856, in the tradition of the annual Feast Day held at this time of the year:

> About Bruton the scenery is very pretty – little dells and rivulets, with deep-cut banks, meeting the eye. The church stands out conspicuously, and was, we believe, the only edifice of its kind on the line on which a token of welcome was hung out. Castle Cary which expects to be largely benefited, made no sign, but at Bruton the arches crossing the line on either side the station were trimmed with evergreens, and bade us 'Welcome to Bruton'.

In Bruton this was 'a day of great rejoicings', the town's folk united in their enthusiasm for honouring this momentous occasion. All the shops were closed and 'trees, laurels, triumphal arches, mottoes, and flags were displayed in every street'. Mottoes included the words 'Victoria', 'Peace, Love and Unity', and, at The Sun Inn, 'Prosperity to Bruton, may its Rail be crowned with success'. The reporter went on to comment on the festivities, which included preparations for the entertainment of 'many hundreds of poor persons'. There was a procession through the town, accompanied by a brass band, followed by a feast on Abbey Green 'where an immense number of men and women were regaled with a substantial dinner of roast and boiled beef, bread, and beer, which, judging from the celerity with which the edibles disappeared, gave infinite satisfaction'. The feast was followed by various traditional sports activities, such as running races and climbing the pole, until late in the evening. In all, about 3,000 people joined in with the festivities, paid for 'by subscription' by tradesmen and others with cash to spare for the purpose of 'making the poor comfortable'. And the sun shone brightly throughout the day.

Just nine years later, in 1865, a terrible accident occurred when a railway worker's failure to reset the points caused a train to career into the sidings and crash into a goods shed. The engine driver, Alfred White, and his fireman, Radford Bartlett, were both killed. The man responsible,

A mid-nineteenth-century sketch of Bruton showing its latest addition, the railway, with a train approaching the station from the west.

James Andrewes, was found guilty of manslaughter and received a prison term of six months. It was probably a different James Andrews, this one of Bruton, who was also sentenced to six months' imprisonment with hard labour for manslaughter. In a drunken fight with his sixty-two-year-old brother, who suffered from weak lungs and heart disease, the brother had died. Although Andrews admitted hitting him a couple of times with a stick it was declared that the wound found on the back of the head of the deceased was sustained when he fell.

Despite the dangers of locomotion, the railway brought great economic and social benefits to the town. For the first time daytrips to seaside resorts, notably Weymouth, Burnham-on-Sea and Bournemouth, became viable for ordinary Bruton families. Annual excursions from Bruton or Cole to such places became annual events for local Sunday Schools and other organisations.

A train enters Bruton Station in the last days of steam.

Some Literary Connections

IN ADDITION TO Bruton's association with the great twentieth-century author John Steinbeck, it has a few more from earlier times which deserve a mention. On the site of the town's library once stood the King's Arms inn, which became the Duke of Wellington Hotel in 1813, two years before the Iron Duke's defeat of Napoleon Bonaparte at Waterloo. This is likely to be the 'principal inn', the 'comfortable country hostel', at which Sir Arthur Conan Doyle's hero arrives in his novel *Micah Clarke* (1889) – a novel revolving around the Monmouth rebellion and the battle of Sedgemoor, fought in mid-Somerset in 1685, just a few miles away from Bruton. He described the 'small country town' as one 'embowered in the midst of a broad expanse of fertile meadows, orchards, and sheep-walks'.

A portrait of the great pirate-navigator and writer-explorer William Dampier (1651–1715), the son of tenant-farmers in the Somerset village of East Coker, hangs in Bruton's King's School Memorial Hall, thus contributing to the attractive tradition that he was once a scholar in

The Duke of Wellington Hotel in the old market-place at the east end of the High Street where the Ward Library now stands.

the town. Unfortunately, his various biographers do not name 'the local grammar school' he attended before going to sea at the age of eighteen. Although there is no evidence that he ever lived in Bruton, let alone, according to legend, buried his treasure in the basement of a house in the High Street, a branch of the Dampier family was, for a time, one of the town's principal landowners during his lifetime. King's School's most distinguished old boy, most would agree, is R.D. Blackmore, the author of *Lorna Doone* (1869) – another tale featuring the battle of Sedgemoor – who attended the school for a year. He was sent there in 1833 with his older brother Henry. 'I do not like it at all,' he remarked in a letter to his aunt on 13 January 1834.

Bruton's Perpetual Curate throughout the 1830s, Stephen Hyde Cassan, was awarded the living of St Mary's in 1831 by Sir Richard Hoare of Stourhead. They shared literary and antiquarian interests and Cassan had lived in the area for many years, serving as a curate in Frome and, subsequently, Mere. In 1829 Cassan was elected a fellow of the Society of Antiquaries and he wrote extensively on a range of ecclesiastical matters including several volumes containing the biographies of successive bishops of Sherborne and Salisbury, Winchester, and Bath and Wells.

Mental illness obliged him to step down from his Bruton post a couple of years before his death in 1841.

A small country town 'embowered in fertile meadows, orchards, and sheep-walks'.

THE HOBHOUSE FAMILY

EVER SINCE HENRY Hobhouse II, an eminent Bristol barrister, purchased Hadspen House in the parish of Pitcombe in 1785 this famous family has made an impact on life in and around Bruton. Henry's father, Henry, together with his brother Isaac, had made his fortune in Bristol as a merchant engaged in the notorious 'triangular trade' in slaves, tobacco and sugar. The many illustrious members of the Hadspen-Hobhouse dynasty include his son, also named Henry, who, as well as being a lawyer and high-ranking civil servant, was an archivist and historian, who helped revolutionise the preservation of public records and state papers. Although he spent much of his working life in London, it was at his Hadspen home that he died in 1854. His son, Edmund, spent part of his life in New Zealand as the bishop of Nelson before, ultimately, retiring to Wells, where he found time to become a very active member of the Somerset Archaeological Society, one of the founders of the Somerset Record Society, and the translator and editor of several medieval texts in the county collection. His younger brother, Arthur, born at Hadspen in 1819, became an eminent judge and received a peerage as Baron Hobhouse. A keen advocate of Victorian-style Liberalism and an anti-imperialist, he supported his niece, Emily, in her campaign to expose atrocities in the concentration camps established by the British in South Africa during the Boer War. He died, appositely, in Bruton Street on Berkeley Square, both these Mayfair place-names deriving from their historic relationship with the place of his birth. Although Emily Hobhouse was born in St Ives in Cornwall, spent many years abroad and did not live at Hadspen, she has given her name to the 'Emily Estate' by which it has been known since it was purchased from the Hobhouse family by the South African business magnate Koos Bekker in 2013. A dedicated social activist and philanthropist who campaigned for the interests of workers, women's rights, refugees, internees and prisoners-of-war, Emily continues to be regarded as a heroine in South Africa for her work on behalf of the Boer people. The name for the complex of hotel and grounds is now The Newt in Somerset.

King's School c. 1948.

Schools

IT IS THOUGHT that there was a grammar school in Bruton as early as 1417. Another, formerly endowed as a Free Grammar School in 1519,

This curious turret feature, built into the Kings School perimeter wall on the bank of the Brue, was commissioned by the headmaster Hoskyns-Abrahall as his personal retreat. It was during his time that R. D. Blackmore was a pupil here. (Photo: Author)

was probably set up a few years before. It survived the dissolution of the Abbey but remained a very minor though locally important establishment, thereafter with an annual average of only twelve pupils during the first quarter of the nineteenth century. The headmaster from 1827 to 1864 was the Reverend John Hoskyns-Abrahall and during his tenure the school was much improved and expanded. From the 1880s it has been known, like others with a similar history, as King's School. By 1897, according to *Kelly's Directory*, the school boasted 'an excellent modern library, containing more than 1,000 volumes, a chemical laboratory, gymnasium, carpenter's shop and new fives courts'. By now it provided an education for about sixty boys. Today King's Bruton is a co-educational independent school with around 340 pupils.

Sexey's School.

Another school, established by the mid-fifteenth century, served the canons of the abbey. John Bishton suggests the room in the upper part of the north tower of St Mary's might have served as a schoolroom. By the middle of the seventeenth century the town had five schools. As well as serving as an almshouse, Sexey's Hospital provided educational opportunities for local boys. In 1791 Collinson remarked, 'the boys are continued in school till they arrive at 14 years and then apprenticed to useful trades, mostly carpenters and blacksmiths'. The school closed in 1877. A new school for the sons of local tradesmen and farmers was founded in 1889, and opened with an initial intake of just fifteen pupils at

'The Glen' in Quaperlake Street while its new premises on Cole Road were being built. In 1897 it comprised a large central schoolroom for fifty boys, a lecture room for thirty boys, a laboratory for twenty boys, workshops, a gym and a staff room. Adjoining the school rooms was the Headmaster's house. In addition, a boarding house for twenty-five boys was provided in Cliff House. Recent additions included a library and a small museum. By now it provided an education for a hundred boys. Sexey's School in the twenty-first century is a non-selective state boarding school for boys and girls aged 11 to 18. Among its notable former pupils are Douglas Macmillan (1884-1969), founder of the Macmillan Cancer Support charity, and the broadcaster, author and entertainer Ned Sherrin (1931-2007).

In the nineteenth century there were several Sunday Schools in Bruton including one at the Congregational Chapel and another at St Mary's. There were also a couple of Dames' schools and, from 1837, a National School for boys. In 1851 a new National School for boys and girls was opened on Silver Street in the vicinity of the former workhouse. This was enlarged in 1895. In 1876 an infants' school was opened on the High Street. This merged with the National School in 1932 to form the council school in new premises on Higher Backway, today's Bruton Primary School.

Bruton's Council School established in 1932, now Bruton Primary.

Sunny Hill School, now known as the Bruton School for Girls.

Established in 1900, Sunny Hill School, now formally known as Bruton School for Girls, was another beneficiary of the Hugh Sexey charitable trust. 'Follow the Gleam', derived from a poem by Alfred, Lord Tennyson, is the inspirational motto for its 200 or so pupils. Its alumnae from local families include Emily Eavis of Glastonbury Festival fame and the well-known columnist and comedian Viv Groskop.

Church and Chapel

In 1776 it can be presumed that the founding hero of the Methodist movement, John Wesley, attracted a great crowd of Brutonians when he preached at the Market Cross at noon on Saturday 7 September 1776. He recorded the reception he received: 'Many seemed to be astonished: all were quiet, and a few deeply affected.' A Methodist Society in the town was promptly established which had nineteen members at the end of 1777. However, the Wesleyan Chapel and its Sunday School did not arrive until the 1840s.

Bruton's churches continued to be well attended. The 1851 census recorded totals of 220 adults and 112 children at St Mary's morning service and another 234 adults and 114 children at the one in the afternoon on Census Sunday. An 'unusually small' congregation of 158 non-conformists in the morning and 285 in the evening met at the Union Chapel on the High Street. In the new Methodist Chapel at West End, built in 1848, fifty adults and thirty-five children attended the morning service and a hundred more adults and twelve children were present in the afternoon. Services were also held at Sexey's Hospital, Wyke and Redlynch.

The West End Methodist Chapel. (Photo: Author)

Special occasions such as the annual Harvest Festivals, introduced around the middle of the nineteenth century, attracted large congregations to church and chapel alike. Despite its generous capacity there was standing-room only for many of those packed into St Mary's to celebrate Thanksgiving in 1881.

Self-help and Philanthropy

For adults in Victorian Bruton, such as the diarist Josiah Jackson, who shared the contemporary enthusiasm of 'self-help' campaigners, there was the opportunity to join the Bruton Institute and Mutual Improvement Society, established in the mid-nineteenth century, and to participate in public debates concerned with such matters as the necessity of war, the continuance of the death penalty, and the controversial notion that smoking might be harmful to health. Series of weekly meetings through the winter presented lectures on a diverse range of topics of contemporary interest including socialism, the rights of women, and the works of Charles Dickens. The society's Reading Room on the High Street (the exact location is unknown) provided printed material including the daily papers. Clergymen and other worthies laid on public 'Penny Readings', attended in large numbers, providing amusement and instruction, not least for the semi-literate and those without the means to purchase books of their own.Several pubs became associated with Friendly Societies in Bruton, the earliest of which was founded in 1760. Friendly societies, organised primarily through their membership subscriptions to raise funds for working men and their families when in need, met at the Sun, the Bell and the Old Bull. This last-named group seems to have been the last to go when it was dissolved in 1914. In 1779 the Bruton Friendly Society had a membership of 101.

In 1841 the newly formed Bruton Freemasons met at the Wellington Inn on the side of the subsequent library. In 1843 they began to use a room in the Sun Inn, built in the 1700s, and by 1864 they were ensconced in the Blue Ball. This exclusive club was dominated by local landowners, professionals and businessmen. On occasion certain skilled artisans were also admitted. Although tradesmen were represented in the gatherings of freemasons, they had their own club, the Bruton Society of Tradesmen, which also held meetings and enjoyed dinners at the Blue Ball and the Wellington. It was active as early as 1815 and emerged again later in the century. Meanwhile the Ancient Order of Foresters met at the Sun and the Blue Ball, and, in the 1840s, a local branch of the Manchester Unity of Oddfellows met at the Old Bull. These were convivial organisations that engaged in a wide range of sociable and communal activities, including parades through the town and Club Day dances and games. In 1879 Bruton's Working Men's Club was established with the encouragement of their middle-class employers.

Philanthropy was as central in Victorian culture as self-help. Numerous philanthropic acts of nineteenth-century Brutonians helped keep their pre-Welfare State society on an even keel. These included grand gestures such as the laying on of feasts and entertainments for dozens, even hundreds, of the poor and elderly. Other benevolent acts included the distribution of blankets, heavily subsidised coal, and fund-raising events such as charity concerts.

The Old Bull on Patwell Street; 'Patwell' is thought to be an abbreviation of 'St Patrick's Well'.

Pubs and Public Amenities

By the early eighteenth century Bruton had at least fourteen inns. Of these, five, the King's Arms, the White Hart, the George, the Swan, and the Unicorn, were located close to the Market Cross in the heart of the town. In 1760 thirteen were recorded, ten of which were on the High Street. Of the town's twelve inns twenty years later, two kept post-chaises. There were just five in 1792 – the Sun, the Bull, the Old Bull, the King's Arms, and the Blue Ball. Prior to its destruction by fire, the Blue Ball site was occupied by the White Hart, dating back to at least 1588. By 1840, however, there were nine, only two of which were deemed 'comfortable'. There were ten in 1881. Beyond Bruton, inns in the locality included the Bear, renamed the Dropping Lane Inn, the Chequers on the north side of

The Blue Ball on Coombe Street as it appeared in the 1920s; along with coaching inns with the same name elsewhere, it is thought to have been named after the practice of attaching a blue ball to a pole outside the inn which, when raised, would advise coach drivers that passengers were waiting to be picked up from the premises.

Shepton bridge, the Three Butchers and the Cock, subsequently known as the Fox, in Redlynch.

Certain improvements were made to Bruton's water supply and drainage services in the 1870s, and in 1896 the Parish Council, formed in 1894, established the Bruton Water Supply company, its piped supply liberating people from the laborious and potentially hazardous business of drawing water from contaminated wells. In 1883 gas-lighting appeared for the first time on Bruton's streets. The gas works of the Bruton Gas and Coke Company were on Shute Lane, in the vicinity of the site of the present stonemasons' workshop. Half a century later, in 1936, electricity arrived in the town.

By the early years of the twentieth century the Council had taken over the responsibility for street cleaning and rubbish collections. Council-funded housing for labourers, built between 1915 and 1917, replaced older cottages on Silver Street. In 1918 the Council first leased Jubilee Park from the trustees of Sexey's Hospital.

Entertainment

THAT FAMOUS PURSUIT of Georgian folk – gambling – was part of Bruton life in the eighteenth century. Horse-racing was a favourite sport for a bet and took place at various venues including Dropping Lane. Parson Woodforde, one of Britain's best-known diarists, was raised in nearby Ansford, close to Castle Cary, and frequently came to Bruton. In 1795 he watched the horse-racing at Burrowfield where 'a vast Concourse of People attended, both gentle and simple'.

Another sport with an antique history enjoyed by men and women in the locality in the 1830s was archery. The ideal Selwood Forest setting for genteel archery conventions was Alfred's Tower, where the long flat sward on the ridge beside it is said to be the length of a bow-shot from the top of the tower. These meetings, so fashionable in the era of the enthusiasm for all things medieval inspired by Scott, Tennyson and others, involved a range of convivial activities including, in the evening, dancing.

Cricket has been played in Bruton since the eighteenth century, possibly earlier. A game associated with the gentry, it was played for pleasure and a decent sum of money by the winning side. In 1772 the Gentlemen of Bruton took on the Gentlemen of Redlynch on a ground close to Dropping Lane in the hope of winning the prize money of 20 guineas. Bruton's Cricket Club had been established by 1858 and, by the 1870s, a town football club had followed. Meanwhile older traditional competition sports, such as violent 'sword and dagger' and 'cudgel-playing' contests, continued to amuse onlookers in and around the town's many drinking establishments. The cruel business of bull-baiting was a further diversion for Brutonians in the eighteenth century; a 'Beautiful Baiting Bull' was advertised for sale at the Bear Inn in Dropping Lane in April 1748, 'to be baited on Easter Monday next'.

In the late eighteenth century Bruton's new Assembly Rooms, now divided into residential apartments, were opened adjacent to the Blue Ball coaching inn at the foot of Coombe Street. As elsewhere these provided space for the local elite to meet for various entertainments, including the playing of cards and dancing.

Victorian-era musical entertainments included performances by the Bruton Philharmonic Society, the Bruton Choral Society (established around 1879), and concerts of both sacred music in church and chapel, and the profane at other venues such as the Assembly Rooms.

In addition to home-grown amusements the town, particularly after the arrival of the railway, attracted a range of touring entertainments. These included displays of exotic animals and performing seals, marionettes and ventriloquists, waxwork exhibitions and circuses. In the spirit of the triumphant European tour of 'Buffalo Bill's Wild West' show, which had recently staged a command performance for Queen Victoria in her Golden Jubilee celebrations in 1887, 'Bortock and Wombell's Wild West' was in town in 1890.

Bruton's former assembly rooms, now Blue Ball Close. (Photo: Author)

A spectacular and daring feat was performed at Bruton's Agricultural Show in October 1892 when the tightrope-walker Pierre Blondin made a visit. Despite his advanced years (he was in his late sixties) he commanded a considerable fee of £150 but, according to Josiah Jackson of Durslade Farm, the show was a success. His two performances that day involved a walk along a rope 200 feet long suspended 60 feet above the ground. The evening show was all the more spectacular with its attendant fireworks as night fell.

One annual celebration in the town that, surprisingly, endures to the present day after hundreds of years, without much evidence of diminishing enthusiasm, is Bonfire Night. In the eighteenth and nineteenth centuries, as now, fireworks were a focus of attention and, sometimes, concern. Great bonfires burned at West End and even on Church Bridge, and children annoyed adults with firecrackers and squibs. One element of the older tradition however has gone: the rolling of flaming barrels, covered in tar, along the town's streets. The custom survives in just one place in the south-west of England, at Ottery St Mary in Devon.

Law and Order

Various parishes in the Bruton hundred had their own constable and tithing-men, elected by a jury of Bruton townsmen. Around the turn of the eighteenth and nineteenth centuries their meeting place for this purpose, each May, was the Sun Inn. The unpaid parish constable had a wide range of civic duties including maintaining roads and bridges, employing a bellman and the watch, and, in times of necessity, billeting soldiers.

By 1897 the town had a police station at West End, which was also home to its professional incumbent, PC Hutchings. The history of the misdemeanours that kept eighteenth-century Bruton's parish constables and Victorian policemen busy is typical of the communities under their watch – a sorry tale of, mostly, petty theft, poaching, drunken brawls, assaults and, occasionally, homicide. Added to this, of course, was the endless round of domestic accidents, suicides, and other catastrophes, including a dismal incidence of drownings, particularly up-river at Batt's Hole, a now much-reduced but, until recent times, very popular swimming spot. One of the more shocking accounts in the annals is that of the brutal murder of an itinerant Irish pedlar, James Wilson, on his way from Wells to Bruton, who was found dead in Creech Hill Lane, beaten to death with a club. His horse was discovered grazing nearby and his pack was also recovered, seemingly hidden in a neighbouring field; so too was the sum of five guineas still safely tucked away in his pocket.

Magistrates held their sessions in Bruton until around 1790. From 1875 the court-house on the High Street was a school for infants before becoming the Masonic Hall, as it has remained to the present day. The pillory, where the convicted paid an uncomfortable public penance for their crimes, stood beside the Shambles on the High Street. It was restored in 1698–99 and replaced with a new one in 1715–16. The town's stocks are also referred to in eighteenth-century records, and it also had a 'cucking stool' which was kept in a close somewhere between the High Street and the river.

In the eighteenth century householders were required to keep buckets of water beside their front doors in the event of fire. There was a serious fire at the Abbey in 1763 and a contemporary letter lamented the fact that if a fire engine had been available 'the damage would have been trifling'. It was not until 1828 that the parish eventually purchased its first fire engine. The Abbey mansion survived until 1786, when it was demolished and its stonework was sold off or given away.

5
BRUTON IN MODERN TIMES

Around and About

In 1953 Bruton had seven inns, two of which took guests; forty-five shops and a population of 1,800. The population remained below 2,000 until the 1980s following a spate of new housing developments. Businesses came and went, the major employers serving the agricultural chain of which the town has always been a part. Examples include Backway Stores, established in 1906, close to Tolbury Mill, which sold a range of commodities including seed, coal, salt and corn. In 1939 milling equipment was set up at Tolbury Mill itself, producing animal feeds until

Aerial view of Bruton between the wars.

Tolbury Mill, now a housing estate developed in the late 1990s.

it was closed in 1989. It was demolished in 1995. Gants Mill, on the other hand, is still a working (water) mill grinding barley and generating electricity. The site of the medieval Abbey mills to the east of St Mary's, now an industrial estate, was converted into a sawmill, warehouses and depot. The Quaperlake bacon factory remained in operation until the 1950s. For a time, the site was occupied by a transport company before being converted into housing. Another major local employer, Provender Mill, closed, after around 150 years, in 1989/90. The Somerset and Dorset Joint Railway, and with it Cole Station, was closed in 1966, a casualty of the notorious Beeching report. The property now named Hillside in Pitcombe was formerly the Railway Inn; the railway viaduct crossing the Brue was destroyed in 1984.

Redlynch House

The early twentieth century marked the passing of a splendid local mansion, Redlynch House, which seems to have been a victim of a defining episode in Britain's early twentieth-century history: that of the Suffragette Movement. Built in about 1708–09, this substantial house had seven principal rooms on the ground floor and fourteen bedrooms above. Servants were housed in the service buildings that were constructed, alongside the stables, close by. The curious gothic archway, known as The Towers, was built in 1755 as part of the then Lord Ilchester's plan to create a grandiose entrance and driveway through his park and ornamental gardens to his mansion. Visitors to the great house included Horace Walpole and also George III during his visits to Weymouth. When Lord Ilchester's son, the second Earl of Ilchester, inherited the estate he turned it back to agrarian use, preferring instead to make Melbury in Dorset his principal residence.

'The Towers' at Redlynch designed by Henry Flitcroft, a principal architect of the structures in the famous lakeside grounds of Stourhead. (Photo: Author)

By 1851 Redlynch House had become a farmhouse. The sixth earl sold the estate in 1912. Only the service range survives, converted into the main dwelling area, probably to the design of Edwin Lutyens, in 1913. The rest of the already dilapidated eighteenth-century mansion was demolished after it was gutted by a great fire in February 1914. In its grounds were found a copy of *The Suffragette* and five incriminating postcards, implying that the fire was an act of arson.

Redlynch House.

Floods

Bruton was once prone to flooding. Serious flooding of houses close to the river was reported at roughly ten-year intervals, in 1866, 1878 and 1888. In February 1900 'The Brue rose rapidly, and by 2 pm all the low-lying parts of Bruton were flooded and the cottagers had to take to their bedrooms.' In 1917 a weather episode gave Bruton the dubious honour of holding a place in the *Guinness Book of Records* until 1955 for being the place with the highest recorded rainfall in the shortest amount of time. Several buildings were destroyed, including dwellings on the south side of the road bridge. A plaque on a wall at the top of Patwell Street records the height of the great flood of 28 June that year when 242.8 mm of rain fell in the space of twenty-four hours and the flood water rose twenty feet or so above the usual level of the river. This was neither the first nor the last of the great floods that afflicted Bruton in its long history. Between 1768 and 1982 the town experienced at least twenty-four major floods. A flood prevention scheme, entailing the construction of the Bruton Dam close to the source of the Brue in 1984, and its improvement in 2008, has, to date, prevented further serious flooding in the town.

Flood damage in 1917; both the Bow Bridge (pictured) and Church Bridge were badly damaged by flooding in 1982.

Bruton at War

King's School's Memorial Hall was opened by the Lord Bishop of London in 1924 to commemorate the fifty-seven old boys who died in the First World War. A reredos was erected in St Mary's for the same purpose and a tablet there commemorates the death in 1916 of Frederick William Norton. The Council-funded war memorial, with its circular pillar and hexagonal plinth, was set up in 1919. The deaths in the Great War of eleven members of the parish of Brewham, and two more during the Second World War, are commemorated on the memorial obelisk in the churchyard of St John the Baptist. Just two names from the First World War and one from the Second appear on the memorial at Yarlington – not quite one of the 'Thankful' villages but close.

Needless to say, the impact of the Second World War, at least as much as the First, was felt by all who lived in and around Bruton between

Dedication service at Bruton's war memorial in 1919.

1939 and 1945. Some fought and died, others mourned and put up with wartime deprivations and inconveniences. Exotic foodstuffs such as bananas and oranges became unobtainable and even local produce was in short supply as, for example, dairies sent much of their milk to Cow & Gate in Wincanton to be processed into powder for the benefit of the nation at large. Dozens of evacuee children arrived in the town, billeted and schooled in Sexey's Hospital and elsewhere. Refugees, such as future Home Guardsman Kurt 'Johnny' Neugasser from Czechoslovakia, aged 16 on his arrival in 1938, added to its increasingly cosmopolitan hue.

In the 1940s Redlynch Park provided a base for the United States Army's 3rd Armoured Division. These Americans, in what was turning into a garrison town, recalls Ken Dominey, 'were a long way from home and sought friendship; this they received in abundance, together with illegitimate children and hasty transfers'. It is said that the famous American heavyweight boxer and then world champion, Joe Louis, 'the Brown Bomber', was one of those stationed at Redlynch and that he coached aspiring Brutonians at Bruton Boys' Club. Locals remember a US army camp on the site of what is now the Tolbury Mill housing estate, then known as the Milk Factory, and also that the Green Guards and the Royal Artillery were in the town for a time, billeted in the old milk factory and nearby Assembly Rooms. Nissen huts and artillery searchlights appeared near Brick Hill Farm on the road to Wyke, and there was an observation post in a dugout close to the Dovecote. Ken remembers that during the Cold War 'a big underground chamber, concrete lined with lead, was dug out on the same site', built as an emergency regional government hide-out which, he maintains, is still there. Redlynch House was one of the D-Day planning centres. It is said that the mangled edges of kerb-stones, marking the passage of American tanks on their way to the D-Day landings, can still be seen along the High Street. In the 1970s a large number of wine bottles and several sticks of American wartime-vintage TNT were found in the investigation and limited excavation of a small building designated a herdsman's shelter abutting Park Wall Road.

Local men in reserved occupations, or exempt from military service for other reasons, comprised Bruton's Home Guard, originally called Local Defence Volunteers. The lives of these members of the Home Guard were in jeopardy – in the event of a successful Nazi invasion it was to be understood that they would not be covered by the terms of the Geneva Convention. Some were members of the Home Guard's Auxiliary Units, a top-secret organisation of hand-picked men trained and equipped to lead the resistance. The local unit had a hidden bunker on Creech Hill which, apparently, doubled as a weapons and ammunition dump. It is said that

Military parade on Bruton High Street in the 1950s.

at the end of the war this was blown up by the Army and a crater near the top of the hill marks its location.

Bruton evaded bombing but the threat was omnipresent. Castle Cary station, down the line from Bruton, was hit and the Railway Inn close by was completely destroyed when a German bomber, pursued by British planes, discharged its load. A signalman and an engine driver lost their lives.

Toward the end of the Second World War, on 10 July 1944, Alfred's Tower was badly damaged when an American plane, on its way to the military airbase at Zeals, crashed into it, killing all five members of its crew. David Green, growing up at Coombe Hill Lodge, recalled how 'Within a few days hardly anything remained of the wreckage' and that 'many local children had taken away many of the pieces for souvenirs'. The finial that was destroyed in the accident was replaced in 1986.

Artist in Residence: Ernst Müller-Blensdorf

Born in the town of Schleswig in north Germany in 1896, Ernst Müller arrived in Bruton after fleeing Nazi Germany in 1933, having been denounced as a 'degenerate' artist, and subsequently escaping from Norway in 1940 at the time of its occupation. Much of his early work, together with his studio, was destroyed. He added the name Blensdorf, becoming Ernst Müller-Blensdorf, when he married Ilse Blensdorf in 1924. They had three children together, Gonda, Eva and Klaus, but eventually separated, divided in their opinions and experience of the Nazi regime. A highly regarded sculptor, Ernst Blensdorf, as he came to be known, had a particular interest in working in Somerset elm, supplied by Snow's sawmill in Bruton. This was a plentiful local material in the decades preceding the ravages of Dutch Elm Disease in the 1970s, and the struggling, unknown (in England) artist could afford it by selecting discarded bases of trunks, damaged by barbed-wire fencing. As his work in the medium developed, his affinity with the twist of the grain grew and helped determine his dynamic, twisting, turning, dancing figures and shapes. He wrote:

> As a rule, I don't know what to do with a piece of wood when I buy it. After its arrival in the studio I usually chop off the bark and the sap wood, and see what shape remains, and how the grain runs ... cleaned off to the dark

BRUTON IN MODERN TIMES

Ernst Blensdorf, 'Refugees' (1940), terracotta, Bruton Museum. (Photo: Dave Watts)

shiny wood itself, the shape is a drama of fight and growth, in spite of all – the wind, the slope it grew on, and the direction of the sun, powerful movements in different directions, and twists – all this gives vitality and an individual life to the tree – and then there comes the moment to ask – What to do with it?.... These vital moving shapes of the tree have to be considered.... It is a slow and tedious process, but you suddenly come to a point where all is won ... it is a splendid moment.

He always used the preservative marketed as 'Cuprinol', made nearby at the company's factory in Frome. Examples of his work and formative sketches are on display in Bruton Museum. As an Expressionist his art is highly subjective: an expression of his inner self, his emotions and values. 'My shapes are never purely abstract', he declared, 'in all my work communication with the onlooker is of great importance.' His subjects included the human form, particularly women and children, and animals, notably seabirds and birds of prey. Some of his work explored biblical themes.

After a spell of internship on the Isle of Man as an 'enemy alien', in 1941 he came, with his three children, to Somerset, teaching art one day a week, Tuesdays, at the Hall School in Bratton Seymour near Wincanton. Here he met his second wife, Jane Lawson, who also taught at the school. Soon he was employed to teach, each Friday in term-time, at Sherborne School for Girls, and, from 1942, at King's School in Bruton. Other places in the locality where he taught for a time included Ansford School on the edge of Castle Cary and a small school for evacuees established at Cranmore.

In 1942 Blensdorf moved to Sheephouse Old Farm on the road between Bruton and Brewham, buying it in a ruinous state for just £500. It is here that some years later, in 1984, Bruton's Anglo-Saxon sword was discovered. He saved the derelict, condemned seventeenth-century building from demolition, restoring it with the help of his sixteen-year-old son, Klaus. He renamed it 'Gladen', which means 'joy' in Norwegian. He and Jane went on to have three more children – Oliver, Carol and Peter, who were raised there.

A committed pacifist, his largest wood-carving, and, in his own opinion, up to that point his best, *Abraham's Sacrifice*, completed in 1951, is eight feet tall. Carved from an elm tree felled at Hazlegrove School, the preparatory school for King's, it depicts Abraham with the body of his

sacrificed son in his lap. In his own words, 'It represents the sum of sculptural ideas and conviction that all the complicated afflictions of men in our time can only be solved by a faith as strong as Abraham's in an ideal.' Inscribed around the base is the message 'Man will be spared great sorrow by faith in the strength of the good'.

The sculpture *Crucifix II*, finished in 1969, is another significant and monumental work, measuring seven and a half feet. Designed to be viewed from below, with an elongated torso and arms, it can be seen in St Mary's Church in Bruton. Since his death retrospective exhibitions of his work have been organised from time to time: one at Christchurch a couple of years after he died, aged seventy-nine, in 1976; another organised by the Royal West of England Academy in 1982; a centenary celebration at St John's Church in Glastonbury and allied exhibitions at several locations in Germany (1996–97); and another, in 2008, organised by Bruton Museum at King's School. This presented the largest assemblage of Blensdorf's work hitherto gathered in one place. A pupil of Paul Klee, and those who have studied his art and published accounts in catalogues and brief biographies, have been unanimous in their assertion that Blensdorf is one of the great modern sculptors and one deserving much wider recognition. It is astonishing that this remarkable and important artist, a naturalised British citizen, is not, at the time of writing, listed in the *Oxford Dictionary of National Biography*.

Ernst Blensdorf, 'Crucifix II' (1969), sycamore, St Mary's Bruton. (Photo: Author)

Writer in Residence: John Steinbeck

ONE OF AMERICA'S greatest and most prolific writers of the twentieth century, John Ernst Steinbeck (1902–1968) is famous for his epic novel of rural deprivation in the United States during the Depression, *The Grapes of Wrath* (1939). He is less well known for his incomplete retelling, a translation into clear, modern, American English, of Thomas Malory's late medieval chivalric romance, printed as *Le Morte d'Arthur* by William Caxton in 1485. Steinbeck's version was edited by Chase Horton and published posthumously in 1976 as *The Acts of King Arthur and His Noble Knights*. It was this book that brought Steinbeck to Bruton in 1959.

Steinbeck began work on his Arthur project in the November of 1956. He expected to spend at least a decade on the

John Steinbeck with American visitor, the artist Betty Guy, at the side entrance to Discove Cottage, his temporary Bruton home in 1959. (Photo: Elaine Steinbeck)

work and regarded it as his most ambitious and important undertaking. His research brought him to England, briefly, in the summers of 1957 and 1958. In the winter of 1958–59 Steinbeck, suffering from a bout of writer's block, decided to make another visit, this time with a view to staying for several months in the mystical 'Vale of Avalon', the traditional Somerset heartland of Arthurian myth. He and his third wife, Elaine, landed at Plymouth in the early spring of 1959. By the end of March that year the Steinbecks had taken up residence at Discove Cottage in the tiny hamlet of Discove, close to Bruton (which, in 1959, had a population of not much more than 1,500). 'It was a fortunate accident which drew me to this place,' he commented to a friend at the time. The playwright and local teacher Robert Bolt, whom they had met on their previous visit, had found the house for the Americans to rent, a short walk through fields and along an ancient track from Bruton, the civil parish of which the communities of Discove and adjacent Redlynch are a part. The centuries-old, two-up, two-down cottage boasted electricity but little else by way of modern conveniences. From here Steinbeck visited South Cadbury hillfort, the legendary location of Arthur's Camelot, and Glastonbury, the 'Isle of Avalon' where Arthur's supposed tomb was found in the grounds of the abbey. Within days of his arrival he was telling friends 'I feel more at home here than I have ever felt in my life in any place.'

Discove Cottage. (Photo: Author)

Although a shy man who tended to avoid company, Steinbeck seems to have made quite an impression on Bruton in his time here – the wealthy New Yorker with the automobile, the employer of local typists, the customer at the Post Office and Mr Windmill's ironmonger's shop. A big man, six feet tall with a barrel chest, large head, broad features, blue eyes, and a neatly trimmed, greying, goatee beard – 'looking like a mildly annoyed lion' according to one reporter – he was a striking figure as he strolled along Bruton's High Street.

John Steinbeck's writing table in Bruton Museum. (Photo: Dave Watts)

Soon after his arrival in Bruton, he ordered a 'table-top architect's board that tilts' because of the pain he felt in his back and neck when leaning over a desk to write. It was made by Admel Drafting Equipment and supplied by Lawes Rabjohns Ltd of Westminster. A few years ago, the same tilting board, kept ever since in store at Discove Manor, was recognised as that commissioned by Steinbeck, and, in 2006, presented to Bruton Museum. Steinbeck mounted it on a card-table and it seems likely that his custom at this stage was to stand as he wrote. His writing implement of choice was a state-of-the-art ballpoint pen mounted in a goose-feather quill.

Steinbeck completed seven chapters of what he intended to be his *magnum opus*. It satisfied neither his literary agent, who doubtless wanted another great contemporary novel, nor the exacting author himself who, ultimately, did not find the voice he searched for during his eight months in Somerset. He left Bruton defeated and depressed – the Grail, mystical and spiritual as Malory's own, had eluded him. Steinbeck never entirely gave up the idea of completing the Arthur book in the remaining decade of his life, nor did he forget Bruton and Discove Cottage where he had found, for a time, true peace and contentment. He paid a last visit to Discove in September 1961, remarking in a letter he wrote the following day in Bruton's Blue Ball Inn, 'The whole thing is like coming home.' To the end of his life he maintained he felt a stronger sense of belonging here than anywhere else he had ever lived: quite a remarkable thing for one whom many consider the quintessential American author.

Modern Times: Change and Continuity

The history of Bruton in the second half of the twentieth century, a period in which other towns in the region, most notably Yeovil, were wholly transformed, is one of conservation and resistance to change. Calls for the development of the Lower Backway for conversion from a cul-de-sac into a main road to take pressure off the increasingly congested High Street were rejected; the town, unlike all its neighbours, is devoid of a hyper-market; major car park construction schemes have failed; and it has retained its main railway station with much improved connectivity with London and elsewhere. The old Post Office, probably built in the eighteenth century and having been derelict for nearly twenty years, was saved from demolition when the Bruton Trust, established in 1970, secured a substantial grant in 1978 to restore it to its former glory. The scheduling of individual buildings is of immeasurable importance in safe-guarding Bruton's historic built environment and the triumph of the campaign for designating the town centre as East Somerset's first Conservation Area has further protected this fragile inheritance. The Manpower Services Commission scheme in 1987 provided the 'Riverside Walk', a popular and convenient landscaped trail running west from Church Bridge. A couple of public art installations – John Sydenham's giant key in the wall of the Community Hall and a sculpture, Giles Penny's *Man on Bench*, opposite – have appeared at its east end in recent years.

In the last quarter of a century Bruton has developed in important ways but mostly the changes have been gradual, even subtle. Housing

The Old Post Office. (Photo: Author)

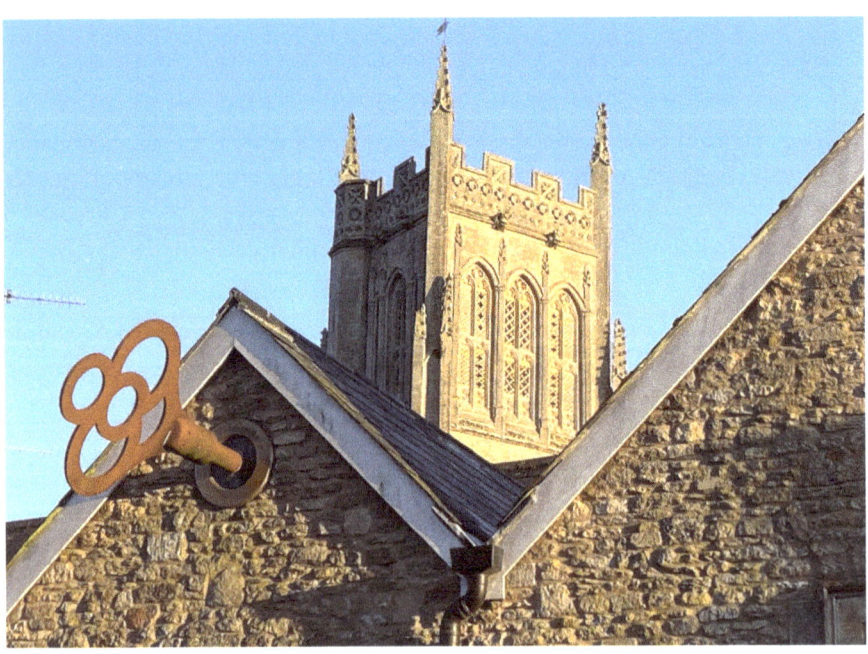

Art installation designed by John Sydenham along the Riverside Walk. (Photo: Author)

developments on the north-eastern side continue to make a significant demographic impact but the town remains comparatively small, with a permanent resident population of just 2,500 in 2017. As taste and styles have changed so have architectural choices and the latest of these, the Cubis estate on the north-eastern edge of the expanding town, makes a bold statement in its modernist design. In recent years, for a variety of reasons, the town has recovered some of its identity as a vibrant commercial centre although the lure of the supermarket in neighbouring towns and the growth of on-line shopping have prevented a full restoration of the wide range of outlets that could be found in the town prior to the 1990s.

The premises of G. W. Fry, constructed in 2012. (Photo: Author)

Climate change concerns and the Covid-19 pandemic have contributed to a growing trend for shopping locally and in other ways supporting local businesses. Attempts to revive the commercial character of the west end of Quaperlake Street, still just visible at the end of the twentieth century, have not flourished but a couple of shops can still be found in Patwell Street, once accommodating the bustling premises of the Co-op. In 1995 Bruton had just four public houses, the Castle, the Sun, the Blue Ball, and the Royal Oak. Only the first two in this list were still open in 2020 prior to

The Cubis development, opened in 2020. (Photo: Author)

the first of the devastating Covid-19 lockdowns, but various other venues have opened and serve a similar role to the pubs and inns of yesteryear. In addition to the ebb and flow of its ever-changing restaurant scene, the town is now served by an interesting range of independent, specialist and boutique stores and a handful of superb 'farm shops'.

Schools remain a defining feature of the town – Kings Bruton and Bruton School for Girls continue to operate as successful independent providers, a Rudolf Steiner school came and went after relocating to Frome, and the primary school thrives as it long has done. Mill on the Brue was established in 1982 and for many years has been a very successful, award-winning, outdoor activity centre for visiting school parties and other groups. Perhaps the single most significant change in terms of local education has been the restoration of Sexey's as a day-school after many years of being exclusively a state-run boarding school. All schools have developed their premises, sometimes in controversial ways, and thus contributed to an ever-evolving townscape. Other local businesses have done the same, most notably perhaps in G.W. Fry's nostalgic constructions on Station Approach harking back to 'the last days of steam' and a Bruton that once was but is no more. A feasibility study, at the time of writing, might lead to the revival of the disused Somerset and Dorset railway line as a walking and cycling path. Bruton's 'Feast Day' tradition has been maintained over the years by church and school fêtes and, from 1999 to

2019, the Bruton Festival of Arts' Packhorse Fair event, held most years on Whitsun Bank Holiday Monday. The town's reputation as a cultural hub and tourist destination, rich in galleries and antique shops, was already well established by the 1980s. Bruton Museum founded at the end of that decade moved to its present location in the Dovecote Building in 1999. Over the years it has developed into a revered community resource for the preservation and celebration of the rich heritage summarized in this book.

The Hauser and Wirth gallery at Durslade Farm in 2020; Durslade was built by the Berkeleys in around 1768 in a period when many more stolid, stone-built farmhouses and outbuildings appeared across the landscape. (Photo: Author)

The extraordinary replica of a Roman villa – the latest visitor attraction at The Newt in Somerset. (Photo: Author)

It cannot be disputed that the single most dynamic development in the area in the last decade has been that of two historic houses and their estates. Durslade Farm, a few years since it was a setting for a major movie, *Chocolat* (2000), has been converted from near-ruin into an internationally renowned arts centre and exhibition space by Hauser & Wirth. Since then the Emily Estate and The Newt in Somerset glorious gardens and hotel at Hadspen have been created – a twenty-first-century undertaking comparable to the development of Stourhead by the Hoares in the eighteenth. Its latest visitor attraction is a full-size replica of a Roman villa, close to where the original, discussed in Chapter 1, once stood. Once again the owners of great estates around Bruton are contributing in myriad ways to its economy and the development of its landscapes. So long as these places remain viable and stay open Bruton's present and future prosperity seems assured. Hauser & Wirth alone was averaging an annual total of 130,000 visitors by 2017. As much as at any time in its long history, Bruton is regarded as a highly desirable place to visit and settle in. This simple fact greatly enhances the prospect of a continuing and developing regard for, and protection of, the precious historic legacy of its cottages, farms and mansions, highways, backways and bartons.

Advertisement for lactic cheese (1931); the cottage on the right has long since been demolished but the local cheese industry continues to flourish.

BIBLIOGRAPHY

Baxendale-Manning, Karen, *Ernst Blensdorf: Sculptor* (Bruton: 1985).
Bedwell, C.E.A., 'Hobhouse, Arthur, Baron Hobhouse (1819–1904)', *Oxford Dictionary of National Biography* (Oxford University Press, 2004).
Benson, J.J., *John Steinbeck, Writer: A Biography* (London: Penguin, 1984).
Bettey, J.H., 'Sexey, Hugh (d. 1619), lawyer and benefactor', *Oxford Dictionary of National Biography* (Oxford University Press, 2006, 2008).
Billings, W.M., 'Berkeley, Sir William (1605–1677)', *Oxford Dictionary of National Biography* (Oxford University Press, 2004, 2008).
Bishton, John, *St Mary the Virgin, Bruton: A Brief History* (Friends of St Mary the Virgin, 2011).
Blensdorf, Oliver, *Ernst Blensdorf, 1896–1976* (Glastonbury: Glastonbury

(Photos: Stuart Anderton)

Arts Festival, 1996).

Boase, G.C., 'Hobhouse, Henry (1776–1854)', *Oxford Dictionary of National Biography* (Oxford University Press, 2004).

Bruton Chamber of Commerce, *Bruton Town Guide* (Bruton: 1984).

Bruton Town Plan Steering Group, *Bruton Town Plan 2017* (Bruton: Mark Pickthall, 2017).

Burchardt, Jeremy, *The Allotment Movement in England, 1793–1873* (Boydell and Brewer, Royal Historical Society, 2002).

Cassidy, I., 'Berkeley, Sir Maurice, 1st. Bt. (1628–90), of Bruton, Somerset and Pall Mall, Westminster', *The History of Parliament: The House of Commons 1660–1690* (Boydell and Brewer, 1983).

Chandler, John, *John Leland's Itinerary: Travels in Tudor England* (Stroud: Alan Sutton, 1993).

Clark, Colin, *A Bruton Camera* (Bruton: Charldon Publications, 1994).

Clark, Colin (ed.), *The Diary of a Wessex Farmer: Josiah Jackson 1882–1904* (Bruton: Charldon Publications, 1996).
Clark, Colin, *Tales from Old Bruton* (Bruton: Charldon Publications, 1998).
Collinson, John, *The History and Antiquities of the County of Somerset* (Bath: 1791).
Costen, Michael, *Anglo-Saxon Somerset* (Oxford and Oakville: Oxbow Books, 2011).
Couzens, Phyllis, *Bruton in Selwood* (Sherborne: The Abbey Press, 1968).
Coxon, Peter, Learmond, Douglas, Saunders, Barbara, *Ernst Blensdorf: A Retrospective Exhibition* (Bruton: Bruton Museum, 2008).
Creighton, Charles, *A History of Epidemics in Britain*, Vol. II (Cambridge: Cambridge University Press, 1894).
Davies, J.D., 'Berkeley, Sir William (1639–1666)', *Oxford Dictionary of National Biography* (Oxford: Oxford University Press, 2004, 2008).
Doyle, Arthur Conan, *Micah Clarke* (London: Longman, 1889).
Dunning, R.W., *The Victoria History of the County of Somerset: Volume VII* (Oxford: Oxford University Press, 1999).
Fleming, Robin, *Britain After Rome* (London: Penguin, 2011).
Fletcher, Robert, *Who's Who in Roman Britain and Anglo-Saxon England* (London: Shepheard-Walwyn, 1989).
Garrard, Bruce, *The River: An exploration of a disconnected river: the Brue and the Axe in Somerset* (Glastonbury, Unique Publications, 2015, 2017).
Guy, Betty, *Surprise for Steinbeck* (San Francisco: Fania Press, 1992).
Harrison, Elaine, 'Hobhouse, Emily (1860–1926)', *Oxford Dictionary of National Biography* (Oxford: Oxford University Press, 2004, 2006).
Hasler, P.W., *The History of Parliament: The House of Commons 1558–1603* (Boydell and Brewer, 1981).
Hayton, D.W., 'Berkeley, John, first Baron Berkeley of Stratton (bap. 1607, d. 1678)', *Oxford Dictionary of National Biography* (Oxford: Oxford University Press, 2004).
Heavey, Philip, Balfour, Elisabeth, Bates, Tim, Learmond, Douglas, *Bruton Remembers, 1939-1945: At Home and Abroad* (Bruton: Royal British Legion, 2005).
Hey, David, 'Fiennes, Celia (1662–1741)', *Oxford Dictionary of National Biography* (Oxford: Oxford University Press, 2004).
Hutton, Ronald, 'Berkeley, Charles, Earl of Falmouth (bap. 1630, d. 1665)', *Oxford Dictionary of National Biography* (Oxford: Oxford University Press, 2004, 2008).
Manning-Sanders, Ruth, *The West of England* (London: Batsford, 1949).
Matthew, H.C.G., 'Cassan, Stephen Hyde (1789–1841)', *Oxford Dictionary of National Biography* (Oxford University Press, 2004).
Mayberry, Tom, Binding, Hilary (eds), *Somerset: The Millennium Book* (Tiverton:

Somerset Books, 1999).
Morris, Christopher, *The Journeys of Celia Fiennes* (London: The Cresset Press, 1947).
Palmer, Marilyn, Neaverson, Peter, *The Textile Industry of South-West England: A Social Archaeology* (Stroud: Tempus, 2005).
Papworth, Martin, *The Search for the Durotriges: Dorset and the West Country in the Late Iron Age* (Stroud: The History Press, 2011).
Pickering, Andrew, Eldred-Tyler, Mandy, *Bruton Through Time* (Stroud: Amberley Publishing, 2012).
Pickering, Andrew, *Steinbeck and the Matter of Arthur* (Bruton: History, Heritage and Archaeology Press, 2019).
Pickering, Andrew, *The Witches of Selwood Selwood: Witchcraft Belief and Accusation in Seventeenth-Century Somerset* (Gloucester; The Hobnob Press, 2021).
Phelps, William, *The History and Antiquities of Somersetshire* (London: 1836).
Randell, P.W., *Stones We Cannot Eat* (Brighton: Pen Press, 2009).
Randell, P.W., *Crime, Law and Order in a Somersetshire Market Town: Bruton c.1500–c.1900* (Brighton: Pen Press, 2011).
Randell, P.W., *Alcohol, Violence, Feasts and Fairs* (Brighton: Pen Press, 2012).
Randell, P.W., *Death Comes to Bruton* (Guildford: Grosvenor House, 2014).
Randell, P.W., *The Life and Times of Hugh Sexey of Bruton: Auditor to James I* (Guildford: Grosvenor House, 2015).
Randell, P.W., *Education in Bruton, Somerset c.1400–c.1900, Vol. 1: The Free Grammar School* (Guildford: Grosvenor House, 2018).
Randell, P.W., *Education in Bruton, Somerset c.1400–c.1900, Vol. 2: Schools for All* (Guildford: Grosvenor House, 2018).
Richardson, Miranda, *An Archaeological Assessment of Bruton* (Taunton: Somerset County Council, 2002).
Sly, N., *A Grim Almanac of Somerset* (Stroud: The History Press, 2010).
Steinbeck, E., Wallsten, R., *John Steinbeck: A Life in Letters* (London: Penguin, 1975).
Steinbeck, John, *The Acts of King Arthur and his Noble Knights* (London: Heinemann, 1976).
Stuckey, John, *A Compleat History of Somersetshire* (Sherborne: 1742).
Sussman, Herbert, *R.D. Blackmore* (Boston: Twayne Publishers, 1979).
Tarbat, A.C., *Bruton* (1956).
Taylor, Stephen, Nolet, Pepijn (eds), *Bruton: An Intimate Urban Ideal* (Bruton: Bruton Museum, 2009).
Underdown, David, *Somerset in the Civil War and Interregnum* (Newton Abbot: David & Charles, 1973).
Vallins, John, 'A grand entrance hints at former splendours: Redlynch, Somerset' in *The Guardian*, 1 April 2013.

Virgoe, Roger, 'Berkeley, Sir Maurice', in Bindoff, S.T., *The History of Parliament: The House of Commons 1509–1558* (Boydell and Brewer, 1982).

Warmington, Andrew, 'Berkley, Charles, second Viscount Fitzhardinge of Berehaven (1599–1668), politician', *Oxford Dictionary of National Biography* (Oxford University Press, 2004, 2008).

Whiting, John, *Persecution Expos'd* (London: 1715).

Winbolt, S.E., *Somerset* (London: G. Bell & Sons, 1929).

Zim, Rivkah, 'Batman, Stephan (c.1542–1584), Church of England clergyman and author', *Oxford Dictionary of National Biography* (Oxford University Press, 2004, 2011).

DR ANDREW PICKERING is the Programme Manager for a University of Plymouth BA (Hons) degree in History, Heritage and Archaeology delivered at Strode College in Street, Somerset. His own undergraduate and postgraduate studies were undertaken at the universities of Birmingham, Keele, Bath and Leicester. He moved from Frome to Bruton in March 1996. He is the author of several local histories including *Steinbeck and the Matter of Arthur: Bruton, Somerset, 1959* (History, Heritage and Archaeology Press), and *The Witches of Selwood: Witchcraft Belief and Accusation in Seventeenth-Century Somerset* (The Hobnob Press). Andrew is chair of the committee at Bruton Museum and his wife, Lisa, is the owner-manager of Ape Or Eden, a small independent bookshop on Bruton's historic High Street.

INDEX

Abbey, Bruton 7, 11, 15–17, 19, 22, 25, 27, 30, 36, 74, 84, 86, 97
Abrahall, John Hoskyns- 73–4
Agar, Margaret 46–7
Aldhelm 10–11
Alfred 12, 14
Alfred's Tower 12–14, 81, 92
Algar 15
Almshouse, Sexey's 40–2, 74
Ames family 26
Amors Barton 18
Andrewes, James 68
Andrews, James 68
Ansford 81, 94
Arthur, Arthurian 7, 96–9

bacon 62–63, 86
Badon, Mount 7–8
Bartlett, Radford 67
Batcombe 35–6, 45–6
Batman, Stephan 28–30
Batt's Farm 15
Batt's Hole 83
Baxter, Richard 48
Beckington 48–50, 52
Bennett, Crystal 4–5
Bennett, Edward 46
Berkeley, earls and family 16, 17, 22, 25, 30–1, 33–6, 38–9, 41, 103
Bernard, Richard 45–6
Bishton, John 74
Blackford 45
Blacklands (Hadspen) 5
Blackmore, R.D. 70, 73
Blensdorf, Ernst Müller- 92–5
Blensdorf, Ilse 92
Blondin, Pierre 82
Bolt, Robert 96
Bratton Seymour 5, 94
Brewham 1, 12, 14–15, 24, 45–7, 53, 57–8, 64, 89, 94
Brownlow, Sir William 35
Brue, River 2–3, 10, 14, 23, 46, 54–6, 73, 86, 88–9, 102
Burrowfield 81

Cadbury, North 52
Cadbury, South (Cadbury Castle) 2–3, 7–10, 97
Camelot 7, 97
Cards Farm 1
Cassan, Stephen Hyde 70
Castle Cary 2, 51, 57, 59, 63, 64, 67, 81, 92, 94
Cenwalh 8
chapels 75–77, 82
church 10–11, 15, 17, 19–20, 22, 46–7, 59, 67, 76–7, 82, 95
Clark, Margaret 47
clothiers 52, 59
clothmaking 23
clubmen 36
Cogley Wood 11
Cole 53, 69, 86
Colinshayes 15
Combe 22, 61
Compton Pauncefoot 45
Conan Doyle, Arthur 69
Cook's Farm 1
Coombes, Margery 51
Cranmore 94
Creech Hill 1–5, 53, 65, 83, 91
Cubis estate 101–2
Cucklington 36

Dampier, William 69–70
Discove 4–5, 96–9
Ditcheat 6
Domesday book 15–16, 22–3
Dominey, Ken 90
Dovecote, Bruton 17, 91, 104
Doyle, Arthur Conan 69
Drogo de Montague 24
Dropping Hill 64
Dropping Lane 1, 58, 61, 79, 81
Durslade Farm 58, 82, 103–4

Eavis, Emily 76
Egbert's Stone 12
Ely, John 38
Evercreech 60, 63

Fiennes, Celia 64
fire 79, 84, 88
Fitzharding, Lord 5, 34, 51
Fitzjames, Sir John 27–8
Flitcroft, Henry 14, 87

foundry 62
Frome 37–8, 45, 48–9, 65, 67, 70, 94, 102
Fry, G W, 101, 103

Gants Mill 23, 61, 86
Gaunt, John le 23
Gilbert, William 16
Gill, A D 54
'Gladen' 94
Glanvill, Joseph 44–5, 48
Glastonbury 2, 7, 52, 76, 95, 7
Godminster 1, 5, 10
Goring, Lord George 34, 36
Green, Alice 47
Green, Catherine 46
Green, Christian 46
Green, Mary 47
Green, David 92
Greene, Richard 47
Greenscombe Farm, Higher 1
Groskop, Viv 76
Grove Farm 6

Hadspen 5, 51, 53, 71–2, 104
Hadspen-Hobhouse dynasty 71
Ham Hill 3
Hardway 53
Hauser & Wirth 58, 103–4
Hazlegrove School 94
Henstridge 57
Henton, John 18
Hoare family 14, 16–17, 57–8, 70, 104
Hobhouse, Emily 72
Hobhouse family 5, 71–2
Holywater Copse 1
Hopkins, Matthew 45
Hopton, Sir Ralph 33
Horton, Chase 96
Hoskyns-Abrahall, John 73–4
Hospital, Sexey's 40–3, 74, 77, 80, 90
Hunt, Robert 45–6, 48
Hussey's Knap 46
Hutchings, P C 83

Ilchester 8–9, 35, 46, 51–2
Ilchester, Lord, 58, 87
Ine 11

Ireson, Nathaniel 22

Jackson, Josiah 77, 82
Jeffreys, Judge 37

Ken, Thomas 36
Kingsettle Hill 14

Lamyatt beacon and temple 4–6, 10
Lawson, Jane 94
Leech, Roger 4
Leland, John 7, 39
lock-up 56
Louis, Joe 90
Lovell family 15
Lusty 40
Luttrell family 15
Lutyens, Edwin 87

Macclesfield 60
Macmillan, Douglas 75
Malmesbury 10
Malmesbury, William of 10
Malory, Thomas 96, 99
manor 14–15, 22, 27, 35, 39, 98
mansions 16, 36, 84, 86–7, 104
markets 22, 38–9, 52, 57, 62–3
market-place 17, 57, 70
Marksdanes 61
Matthews, Samuel 33
Melbury Sampford 87
Methodists 76–7
mills 22–23, 59–61, 85–6
Milton Clevedon 2, 15, 53
Mohun, William de 15, 16
Molland, Alice 48
Molton, South 41
Monmouth, Duke of 34, 37–8, 69
Montagu, Montacute, de, family 24
Mount Badon 7–8
Müller-Blensdorf, Ernst 92–5

Neugasser, Kurt (Johnny) 90
North Cadbury 52
Norton St Philip 37
Norton, William 89

Oglethorpe, Theophilus 37
Ottery St Mary 83
Over Stowey 60

Papworth, Martin 3
Parker, Matthew 30
Patwell, Patwell Street 16–17, 54, 62–3, 79, 88, 101
Pen Pits 2
Penselwood 2, 8, 10, 12, 38
Phelps, William 5
Phillips, Sir Edward 51–2
Pitcombe 2, 6, 23, 53, 71, 86
priory, Bruton 15–18, 24, 49
Provender Mill 86

Quakers 51–2, 59
Quaperlake, Quaperlake Street 17, 39, 49, 60–3, 75, 86, 101
quarrying 16, 61

railway 59, 67–8, 82, 86, 92, 99, 104
Randell, Peter 24, 26
Redlynch 1, 23, 25, 27, 39, 53, 65, 77, 80–1, 86–8, 90–1, 97
Redmore 46
Romano-British period 2, 3, 6, 10
Russell, Thomas 30

Saxey family 41
Saxon period 7–11, 15, 60–1
schools 3–4, 17, 27–8, 30, 41, 45, 56, 69–70, 72–6, 83, 89, 94–5, 102–4
Scobell, Captain 58
Sedgemoor 34, 37–8, 69–70
Selwood 3, 7–8, 12, 30, 44–5, 81
Sexey, Hugh 40–2, 45, 76
Sexey, William 41
Sexey's Almshouse 40–2, 74
Sexey's Hospital 40–3, 74, 77, 80, 90
Sexey's School 74–5, 103
Sexeye, Robert 24
Shakespeare, William 30
shambles 39, 84
Sheephouse Farm 11, 94
Shepton Mallet 38, 52
Shepton Montague 2, 24, 38
Sherborne 7, 10, 70, 94
Sherrin, Ned 75
shops, shopping 62, 65, 67, 74, 85, 97, 101–2, 104
silk, silk-throwing 58, 60–1
Smallcombe Hill 53
Smalldown 2
South Cadbury (Cadbury Castle) 2–3, 7–10, 97
South Molton 41
Spicer, William 48, 49

Stanton, William 41
Steinbeck, John 3–5, 69, 96–9
Stoke Trister 45
Stourhead 14, 16, 22, 57, 70, 87, 104
Stourton 12
Stowey, Over 60
Swanton House 40–1
Swing, Captain 57
Sydenham, John 99, 100
Syms, Joan 47

Tabor, Richard 2
Talbot, Elizabeth and Joseph 47
Tancarville family 15
Taunton 34, 37, 51
Tennyson, Alfred, Lord 76, 81
Tolbury House and Mill 61, 85–6, 90
tolls, tollhouse 65, 66
turnpike 38, 64–6

Uphills 17
Upton Noble 53, 61

Virginia 27, 32–3
Vowles, Richard 27

Walpole, Horace 87
Walter, Henry 47
Warbeck, Perkin 24
Warberton, Dorothy 47
Warberton, Mary 46
Ward, George 60
Ward, John Sharrer 58, 60–1, 70
Wesley, John 76
Westfield 22
Westonzoyland 37
Whaddon House 61
Whitehead, Thomas 52, 59
Williamsburg, Virginia 32–3
Wilson, James 83
Wincanton 22, 34, 36, 38, 48, 56–7, 59, 63–4, 90, 94
Witches, witchcraft 44–6, 48–51
Witchfinder-General 45
Woodforde, James 81
Wyke Champflower 10, 25, 53, 77, 91

Yarlington 6–7, 53, 89

Zeals 92

www.ingramcontent.com/pod-product-compliance
Lightning Source LLC
Chambersburg PA
CBHW050016090426
42734CB00021B/3295